CHRISTIAN
REALISM AND
PEACEMAKING

Christian REALISM &PEACE-MAKING

ISSUES IN U.S. FOREIGN POLICY

RONALD H. STONE

ABINGDON PRESS
NASHVILLE

CHRISTIAN REALISM AND PEACEMAKING
ISSUES IN U.S. FOREIGN POLICY

Copyright © 1988 by Abingdon Press

This book is printed on acid-free paper.

Library of Congress Cataloging-in-Publication Data

Stone, Ronald H.
   Christian realism and peacemaking.

   Includes index.
   1. Peace—Religious aspects—Christianity.
   2. Civil rights—Religious aspects—Christianity.
   3. United States—Foreign relations—1945–
   I. Title.
BT736.4.S76   1988   261.8'17   88-10512
ISBN 0-687-07572-6 (pbk.: alk. paper)

Scripture quotations except where noted are from the Revised Standard Version of the
Bible, copyright 1946, 1952, 1971 by the Division of Christian Education of the
National Council of the Churches of Christ in the USA. Used by permission.

Scripture quotations noted NEB are from The New English Bible. © The Delegates of
the Oxford University Press and The Syndics of the Cambridge University Press 1961,
1970. Reprinted by permission.

Portions of chapter 2 were originally published in "Christian Realism and Peacemaking" in
the Fall 1982 issue of *Review and Expositor.*

Portions of chapter 5 were originally published in "The Justifiable War Tradition" in
The Peace-making Struggle (Lanham, Md.: University Press of America, 1985).

MANUFACTURED BY THE PARTHENON PRESS AT
NASHVILLE, TENNESSEE, UNITED STATES OF AMERICA

To
Patricia and Randall
May they be blessed as peacemakers

CONTENTS

Preface...9

I. Peacemaking and War.................................17
   The Present Danger................................ 17
   The Theological Dimension......................... 19
   Toward a Definition of Peacemaking............... 23
   The Origins of War............................... 26

II. Christian Realism and Peacomaking 33
   Christ and Caesar................................ 34
   Christian Realism and the Cold War............... 36

III. The Ethics of Peacemaking....................... 48
   Faith Not Idolatry............................... 48
   Hope Not Armageddon.............................. 55
   Hope Inspires Action............................. 58
   Active Love Seeking Peacemaking.................. 61
   A Just Peace..................................... 63

IV. Realism, Human Rights, and Foreign Policy............. 66
   Universal Standards in Ninth Century B.C.......... 68
   Other Sources.................................... 70
   The Modern Situation............................. 71
   The Nomination of an Assistant Secretary of
       State for Human Rights....................... 73
   Niebuhr on Human Rights.......................... 74
   The Carter Human Rights Attempt................. 77
   Ernest W. Lefever and Human Rights............... 80
   The U.N. Human Rights Commission............... 83

V. *The Justifiable War Tradition*............................86
    Augustine of Hippo......................................87
    Thomas Aquinas.. 90
    John Calvin.. 92
    Application to Our Time............................. 93
    The Catholic Bishops................................. 96
    The United Methodist Bishops, 1986................97
    The Strategic Defense Initiative...................... 98

VI. *Revolution and Counterrevolution in Central America* 102
    Ambiguity and Antirevolution........................103
    Nicaragua and El Salvador......................... 105
    Struggle in the Churches............................ 109
    Alternative Models.....................................119

VII. *Development: The Indian Example*......................122
    Forces Resisting Development...................... 129
    Action for Development.............................132

VIII. *Response to Religious Roots of Terrorism*.................138
    The Shiite Crusade...................................141
    A Christian Realist Response........................145
    What Is to Be Done?................................ 147

IX. *Relations with the Russians*...............................151
    More Than Forty Years Without World War.... 153
    The Era of Gorbachev...............................156
    Foreign and Military Policy......................... 160

X. *Toward a Relevant Church Policy*........................ 165
    A Variety of Churches................................166
    Political Action and Resistance...................... 171

Notes.. 177

Index of Scriptural References............................ 187

General Index...189

PREFACE

The purposes of this book are to clarify the peacemaking tendencies of Christian realism and to deepen the ethical reflections underlying the American churches' contribution to U.S. foreign policy. Peacemaking can disintegrate into sentimentalism if not engaged with realism. Christian realism can be made into an ideology of reaction if not informed by peacemaking.

I write from within the traditions of the emerging Christian peacemaking work and from within the tradition of Christian realism's reflection on U.S. foreign policy. Although I recognize the two traditions are sometimes estranged, I reject the idea that the two are antithetical. A tough-minded peacemaking and a compassionate Christian realism are synonymous.

The book is within both a tradition and a personal modification of that tradition. Earlier realists Reinhold Niebuhr, Hans Morgenthau, George Kennan, and John C. Bennett had their formative judgments of Russian communism shaped by Stalin.[1] To varying degrees they changed their judgments of the Soviet Union after Stalin's death. Stalin's death is one of my first political memories; so I do not need either to criticize these Christian realists for their judgments about Stalinism or to remain at the place where their pre-Khrushchev polemics were. Sometimes I think two thirds of the critique of Christian realism are derived from a failure to recognize its evolution. Some neoconservatives remain at the level of anti-Stalinist polemics, and other left-of-center critics attack realism for ever having an anti-Russian communism polemic. So the book represents Christian realist thinking during the Brezhnev-Gorbachev period of U.S.-Soviet relations. It is of the nuclear age and the age of Third World development and liberation struggles. Christian realism evolves.

Christian realism in the United States was born in the struggle with twentieth-century totalitarianism. Its first struggle was against fascism, and it took on its shape from the need to strengthen democratic thinking for the struggle with Nazism. Reinhold Neibuhr pioneered in liberating American Christian thinking from pacifism and isolationism. A German-Jewish refugee, Hans J. Morgenthau, developed his philosophy of international relations out of the struggle with Nazism and the resultant conflicts with the Soviet Union's communism. Its foremost diplomatic historian, George Kennan, was declared *persona non grata* by the Soviet Union, and his ambassadorship to that country was ended in 1952. Obviously a worldwide rivalry with the Soviet Union continues in the late 1980s. To a large degree the foreign policy recommendations of this group sought the security of the United States. The realities of the weapons of planetary destruction make seeking security in the late twentieth century a peacemaking work. National security now requires cooperation with foes to manage the dreaded weapons, which bring the earth close to the brink of destruction.

I hope this stage of the evolution of Christian realism can inform peacemakers, Christian or secular. It is important to stand within an ethical tradition. American social-Christian thought lost a lot by its premature burial of Walter Rauschenbusch. Neoconservative interpretations of Christian realism may lead many to want to bury it. But it is better procedure to free Christian realism from the claims the neoconservatives make, and use the tradition for peacemaking rather than for the Soviet-bashing attitudes of the neoconservatives.

The book itself does not deal directly with all the critics of Christian realism. It rather joins realism with Christian peacemaking and therein presents a case for the tradition's own persuasiveness. I have responded to some critics elsewhere and will in the future respond to other critics, but the book argues for an evolution of the tradition. None of the current alternative social-ethical traditions offers alternatives strong enough for the center of Christian social thought to risk a paradigm shift to new models. The social cruelties of the neoconservative movement in Christian thought, with their apologies for militarism, South Africa's apartheid, and Somocista counterrevolution, do not have to threaten the center of American Christian social ethics. The concerns of the liberation movements are seen as necessary correctives of provincialism in the tradition. The neofundamentalism support of rightwing tendencies in American

Christian thought is socially powerful when allied with the neoconservativism, but it holds no respectable intellectual position and consequently will fade. The peacemaking of Christian realism can be put to work in the American churches and in the process contribute to peace. Consequently, the book concludes by discussing putting peacemaking to work.

The 1980s have seen a deepening and an expansion of the churches' involvement in peace and justice ministries. To some degree this is true of all churches. The realities of the arms races, the frequency of wars, and the increased attention to the problems of poverty and starvation have had an impact on all churches. The World Council and the National Council of Churches have expressed these concerns. The denominations in the United States have returned to the peace and international justice issues with a commitment that waned for a few years after the Vietnam war.

This return to the peacemaking and justice issues has reopened the debates over acceptable moral strategy vis-à-vis weapons of mass destruction. The consensus that formed in Protestantism around the acceptability of the strategy of nuclear deterrence has begun to come undone and the debate has been renewed.

Another significant factor in the new debate has been the increased attention paid to spokespersons for Third World churches. The demands have been made that justice issues are indissolvably connected with peace issues. This has meant that the peace issue debate in the churches is related to issues of international economic justice. It has also meant that the Christian sympathy for liberation struggles has prevented the Christian desire for peace from being expressed in absolute pacifism. Justice and peace are seen as linked in the meaning of *shalom* even though there may, in some cases, be a tension between justice and order.

This movement of the churches toward deeper engagement with the peace and justice issues is seen in the 1980 policy of the Presbyterian Church entitled *Peacemaking: The Believer's Calling.*[2] It was a policy statement of the United Presbyterian Church (U.S.A.), which was adopted by the Presbyterian Church (U.S.), creating a program of education and action priority for the whole church. As the two major Presbyterian churches united they began another discussion in committee around the themes of resistance to war, while the whole denomination increased its work under the guidance of the Peacemaking Program. The United Methodist bishops led their denomination with a statement for discussion and action, *In Defense of Creation: The Nuclear Crisis and a Just Peace*,[3] in 1986. The United Church of Christ redefined their church as "A Just Peace Church" in 1985 and began to work toward that mission with the publication of *A Just Peace Church*[4] in 1986.

A statement that made even greater public impact than the statements of the Protestant bodies was the 1983 United States Catholic bishops' pastoral letter on war and peace, *The Challenge of Peace: God's Promise and Our Response*.[5] All these statements defined the concern for peacemaking as a theological priority. Together with the statements, education, and actions of other denominations, they have raised the public's consciousness of a significant church peace movement.

Traditional "Peace churches," whose roots are in the history of Christian sectarian pacifism, have also experienced a new burst of energy regarding their peacemaking work. The 1986 commitments of the Brethren Church to a complete program of peace education and political action for peace is an example of this energy. The "Brethren Resolve for Peace" admits the different approaches to peace that characterize the denomination, but moves ahead on a program of action. The Brethren too seem to be moving beyond the debates between Christian realists and total pacifists to active social engagement for peacemaking.[6]

All these shifts in priorities are due in the 1980s for further discussion and actions in their respective churches. The goal of this study is to engage this evolving church search for peacemaking with the evolving tradition of Christian realism, hoping for their mutual enrichment and synthesis. I think each chapter will reveal development beyond positions often attributed to Christian realism.

There are many problematic areas in international affairs other than the ones I have chosen. In regard to geographical regions, I have limited myself to regions of the world with which I have some limited firsthand experience. In regard to intellectual problems, I have not repeated discussion of national interest, power, just-war theory, and revolution, which were discussed in *Realism and Hope* (1977); I trust the problems discussed briefly here—peacemaking ethics, development, human rights, terrorism, and Soviet-U.S. relations—will illustrate the fruitfulness of joining realism and peacemaking.

Several opportunities have contributed to the realization of the book. Two courses at Pittsburgh Theological Seminary, "The Ethics of

Peacemaking" and "Church and Society in International Perspective," have fed thought and student dialogue into the work. The peacemaking work of the Presbyterian Church has involved me over the last decade and provided opportunities for study and dialogue in the United States and abroad. Primary inspiration has been from the work of the Advisory Council on Church and Society.

Two chapters have appeared elsewhere in shortened forms. Both have been updated, revised, and lengthened to become parts of this study. Appreciation and acknowledgment is extended to the previous publishers: *Review and Expositor* (Fall 1982), edited by Glen Stassen, for chapter 2; and University Press of America, for chapter 5, from *The Peacemaking Struggle* (1985), edited by Dana Wilbanks and myself. Chapter 4, on human rights, is an expanded version of an unpublished paper delivered to the Society of Christian Ethics in January 1982. I benefited at the time from the critique of Michael Novak, the United States Representative to the Human Rights Commission. Professor Novak represents the neoconservative perspective debt to Niebuhr. I hope this chapter in its revised form will illuminate the human rights issues as well as demonstrate how the neoconservatives have misunderstood Christian realism. Of course, much worse than misreading the tradition is their support of the debasement of human rights in Central America and South Africa and their attack on human rights in domestic politics.

Five chapters were written in India on a sabbatical in 1985 provided by Pittsburgh Theological Seminary and assisted by a grant from the Association of Theological Schools, and rewritten in Pittsburgh in 1986–1987. The United Theological College graciously provided accommodations and community for me, my wife Bebb, and the children, Randall, Jessica, John, and Patricia, in Bangalore, India. A special word of thanks is due to Bebb, who urged our family on to India despite Indira Gandhi's assassination, the massacres of the Sikhs, the Bhopal atrocity, and the communal violence of India in 1984–1985. The book reflects that ethos, and without her courage my mind would have missed the Indian happenings of that year. Chapters 8, 9, and 10 were written in the United States in 1987.

An invitation to deliver the Niebuhr Lectures at Elmhurst College in April 1987 permitted the discussion of several topics around the lecture series subject, Christian Realism and U.S. Foreign Policy.

Of the two dozen Christian peacemakers whose contributions are woven into this work, I would thank especially Dana Wilbanks, Dean Lewis, and Robert Smylie for their intellectual and practical assistance over this last decade. Their respective vocations are outstanding examples of Christian peacemaking action.

Pittsburgh, 1987

CHRISTIAN REALISM AND PEACEMAKING

I. PEACEMAKING AND WAR

The Present Danger

The two friends say farewell with a hug and a blessing of *shalom* at the Prague airport. Between them personally, *shalom* is real, but between their nations of Czechoslovakia and the United States, it is absent. I had come to Czechoslovakia twice in the last year to preach, lecture, and engage in dialogue on peace with Christians and with Marxists. The friend saying farewell at the airport had come to the United States to build bridges between his peace organization and American churches. The salutation *shalom* reaches deep into our human need for peace and justice. Yet at the Prague airport the difficulty of realizing peace and justice and the dangers of reaching for the illusion of peace are remembered.

On the surrender of Czechoslovakia to the armies of Hitler, the Western and Soviet alliance containing Germany foundered in 1939. Neville Chamberlain's promise of "Peace in Our Time" was an illusion, and the Munich peace has become a symbol among the allies of false appeasement. The Russian armament dominating Czechoslovakia reminds us still of that false peace of forty-five years ago.

A Christian pilgrim in Bethlehem meeting an armed Israeli patrol will have his greeting of *shalom* eagerly returned by the young Israelis. The ironies in Bethlehem run deep; *shalom*, a greeting like Good Morning, is also a promise that some day order in Bethlehem will not depend on armed patrols amid the hostility of a defeated population. Peace is there in the intentions of many of the people. It is present in the religious hopes of those faiths that divide Jew, Christian, and Moslem. The reality is only an armed truce covering resentments, remembered injustices, and human hostilities temporarily repressed. The pride in the faces of the Israeli patrol hides their own insecurity.

17

Their military prowess has led them to dominate the skies over Cairo, Baghdad, Damascus, Ammon, and Beirut. In their daring attacks they have outdone King David as they have rolled into Egypt, Jordan, Syria, and Lebanon. Yet they have overtaxed themselves; they cannot afford the military machine they have created. Americans must pay for it. Israel cannot protect captured populations, and Christian revenge stains the Israeli army's honor. Peace eludes victorious Israel. Is peace to be regarded as only a pious wish, a hope, or an illusion in today's world?

Militarism is on the rise. It is seen in the inability of the major powers to slow down the arms race. The arms traffic among the smaller powers also continues to grow. Their appeals to the super-powers to freeze the arms race are hardly heard as they hurry to arm themselves with weapons they cannot afford. The presence of large armies inclines leaders to rely on them rather than on diplomacy. The vast sums of money available for arms purchases tend to promote corruption within the government. The training needed to manage sophisticated weapons systems tends to produce a privileged military elite. Learning, research, and expertise tend to follow resources, and the hold on society of military leadership increases. Arms races tend to perpetuate themselves so that one side's gain is the other's loss, which must be compensated for by escalating armaments. Pakistan and India present a classic case of developing nations feeding their poverty by countering each other's weapons acquisitions.

Militarism is on the rise not only in increased armaments, but in the vicious wars of the late twentieth century. Recently, wars in Latin America have raged from the Malvinas to Nicaragua and Grenada, and in insurrections throughout the land. In Asia, a major conflict rages between Iran and Iraq, and war goes on in Cambodia, Afghanistan, and Lebanon. In Africa, war in the former Spanish Sahara, in Chad, in Ethiopia, in Namibia, and various military coups, has kept the continent in turmoil. Each of the major powers—the United States, the Soviet Union, the United Kingdom, China, and France—has committed part of its armed forces to action during recent years. Every power that admitted to possessing nuclear weapons engaged in warfare with conventional weapons. In the case of China and the Soviet Union, they fought on their troubled borders. The United Kingdom, France, and the United States fought in the former colonies of Europe in America and Africa.

Probably the greatest threat to the prestige of militarism came about by the focus on the doomsday quality of nuclear warfare. Research drove into the popular consciousness, in a way it had not before, that the human experience on earth could be ended through war. The dreaded promise of nuclear winter, an earth atmosphere so full of smoke, debris, and dust that nothing could grow, became accepted as a probable outcome of limited nuclear war. Plans to defeat the enemy were seen as self-defeating. Nuclear war came to bear more and more the character of omnicide. Jonathan Schell's *Fate of the Earth* had a shaking impact in the United States[1] and Carl Sagan's research fell into minds prepared to believe that nuclear war could end the human drama.[2] The disaster of Chernobyl pricked the conscience of a nuclear-addicted world.

The ultimate character of these weapons with which we are arming ourselves is that which makes the struggle for peace a theological issue. Our present policy threatens to end humanity. A question of humanity's being or nonbeing has emerged.

The Theological Dimension

The awareness of the nearness of the nuclear apocalypse is worldwide. Human minds are forced to deal with the terror and with reducing the terror. No matter what other human concerns are present, the concern about the end of humanity is present. It absorbs other threats, it promises to reduce all other human achievements to nothing. Human finitude is now obvious. All are bound together in their finitude, facing the obliteration of the human species and all of the institutionalized memory of humanity. The confrontation with nonbeing is no longer a conclusion of philosophy, but a shocking recognition of the conditions of all human existence.

The criteria of theology as articulated by Paul Tillich required that the question of peace be at the center of his theological system. He never quite saw the implications of his definitions. The first formal criteria of his theology was:

> The object of theology is what concerns us ultimately. Only these propositions are theological which deal with their object in so far as it can become a matter of ultimate concern for us.[3]

The only question that deserves ultimacy for humanity, once the question itself has appeared, is the question of the end of humanity.

To put it simply, Tillich argues that the ultimate question is the center of theology, the ultimate question is the survival of the human race; therefore, the survival of the human race is the center of theology.

Theology is a human endeavor. It is human thinking about God's relationship with humanity. There was a time when the universe was without humanity. In all probability there will be such a time again. But there will be no human theology without humanity, so the survival of the human species becomes central to theology. To recognize the humanness of theology is not to displace God from the theology. It is not to make the universe dependent on humanity. It is simply to recognize that humanity's purpose seems to be to love God, and that theology as a way of loving God must, out of love of the neighbor, engage in preserving the human species. Tillich has suggested that the content of the ultimate question has shifted through history. Tillich projected his systematic theology in the 1920s and he wrote it in the '50s. It bears the marks of these years of existentialism. Under the pressures of political failure and European collapse, his thought focused on the human suffering of the European-American psyche.

> It is not an exaggeration to say that today man experiences his present situation in terms of disruption, conflict, self-destruction, meaninglessness and despair in all realms of life.[4]

From this perspective he remembered that the question of the early Greek church had been the issue of "finitude of death and error." The question of the Reformation church had been that of a "merciful God and the forgiveness of sins." Modern Protestantism had turned either to Jesus as the personal ideal of human existence or to the kingdom of God as the Christianization of society. The Roman Catholic Church had tended to see the message of the gospel in "salvation from guilt and disruption by the actual and sacramental sacrifice of the God-man."[5] Today we can see more clearly than could Tillich the source of meaninglessness; it is the threat of nonbeing of the species.

Similar conclusions follow from examining Gustavo Gutiérrez's periodization of the central questions of theology. He too knows that theological study has taken on different tasks in history. He believes that in its early history theology was essentially reflection on the Bible for the development of the spiritual life. Its goal was the perfection of the ascetic life. From the twelfth century on, he sees a division in theology, with rational knowledge as its goal gradually superseding spiritual guidance. Gradually he thinks theology disintegrated into its systematic and defensive roles and lost its role as reflective reason. In the present, he finds theology reactivating its practical role. The current emphasis is that of "theology as critical reflection on Christian praxis in the light of the Word."[6] This shift gives his theology a decidedly practical edge. It allows the enlistment of social science to theology in a manner that has characterized Protestant use of social science in social ethics. As the priority of the poor emerges in liberation theology it becomes critical reflection on church life for the empowerment of the poor. It becomes hard to distinguish theological statements from ideological statements of particular political parties. The struggle for being may be carried by particular parties, but theology is more than the program of those parties. Tillich pointed to the need to define theology in terms of the rationality of the universal as well as the existential immediacy.

> Our ultimate concern is that which determines our being or non-being. Only those statements are theological which deal with their object in so far as it can become a matter of being or non-being for us.[7]

Being here means the whole of human reality. Tillich knew of the disruption of this human reality. He knew that its disintegration threatened human existence. He did not yet know in the 1950s what every child now knows: that it can all be literally blown away. His words point to the moving of the peacemaking concerns to the center of theology. The peacemaking reflection of theology is that which concerns ultimate matters. The question of being and nonbeing is an immediate question of theology. Nonbeing loses its vague connotations; it means simply destroying the meaning of that which is. Being is the humanly understood reality that supports life; nonbeing is its opposite.

Obviously many types of theological emphasis have emerged in the modern period. Particularly, liberation theologies have resisted forces of nonbeing for the particular groups whose causes they have espoused. Women's liberation theology, Third World theologies of liberation, and black liberation theologies have all resisted nonbeing. Work in Christian bioethics, business ethics, and Christian political ethics has also shared in reflecting on practical ways to combat forces of disintegration. All of these theological specialties have insights to contribute to the central theological task: the making of peace. To the extent that these specialties neglect to relate their work to peacemaking they will be partial and unfulfilled. Similarly the central task of theology, reflecting on the meanings and conditions for peace, cannot proceed without the detailed work of the current emphases. It should be clear that there cannot be peace without liberation from oppression. Peace cannot be achieved without just political economies and the regulation of life sciences. This study moves into specific reflections on human political practice. At this level the engagement is with observations and methods grounded in social ethics. No sharp line can be drawn between Christian theology and Christian social ethics. Social ethics is more concerned with analyzing social policy. Theology is more concerned with the ultimate frame of reference for the social policy. That all social policy should promote peace is a theological concern. Whether unilateral or multilateral forms of economic aid better serve peace is a question for social ethics. As the questions of social ethics approach questions of being and nonbeing they become theological. There is a continuum of method and subject with the social ethical questions of preferable policies shifting into concerns that are appropriately theological. Social ethics is broader than theology, though; social ethics draws on non-Christian sources, its analysis ranges beyond the theological circle. The theological circle has a particular tradition confessing particular answers to general questions. Social ethics could perhaps conclude that there is no answer to the human search for peace. If theology were driven to confess that its answers to the search for the preservation of being were inadequate, it would confess the inadequacy of the theological circle itself.

Paul Tillich began writing his systematic theology in a tower of Union Theological Seminary across Broadway from the offices of the Manhattan Project, which directed the manufacture of the first nuclear device. He completed the system at the University of Chicago where the first controlled atomic reaction was achieved. These technical events have changed theology. The words about God, the very words taken from early Greek theology, from the myths of creation in Plato, came to have new potent significance. Nonbeing is no longer primarily a realm out of which God created order. It is the threat of nothingness against the very imperfect order that supports human life. It is a commonplace assumption that our technological mastery has outrun our moral imagination. We have not yet faced the theological implications of this destructive power. As the designers of the first atomic explosive reacted with awe to the power they had created, and named the site of their explosion "Trinity," they unknowingly faced the redoing of Western theology. If nonbeing in a nonhuman environment is the fate of the earth, what does the power of God mean? If sin leaves us with nuclear-armed enemies threatening one another, what does grace mean? Is the meaning of human freedom restricted to the freedom to destroy, or may it contain possibilities of reversing the drift into destruction? The radical challenge to theological vocabulary results from the technological change. The reality of one weapon system, whether an airplane or a submarine, having more destructive power than all the destructive power unleashed by the hatred of 1939–1945 changes our frame of reference. It forces people to think of ultimates, of being or not being. The hatred of 1939–1945 spawned the bomb; the legacy of 1939–1945 ensured that the bomb would be developed to its present leviathanlike threatening posture.

The present flurry of writing on peace-related themes has still not produced an agreed-upon meaning of peacemaking for Christian use. The term in Scripture is very broad, and until recently the reflection in Christian theology on peace ethics has been less than the focus on the ethics of war.

Toward a Definition of Peacemaking

Two of the great religious encyclopaedias published just prior to World War I reveal in their attitudes toward the subject of peace the need for a contemporary definition. *The New Schaff-Herzog Encyclopaedia of Religious Knowledge*, published in 1910, did not contain an essay on the concept of peace. It did however have a knowledgeable essay, "Peace Movements," by Benjamin F. Trueblood, Secretary of the American Peace Society, Boston. After surveying the gains of the peace movements in the nineteenth century, he concluded:

> One is compelled to believe that the permanent peace of the world is no longer merely an ideal and a dream. The conclusion is unescapable that the world has already entered upon the practical realization of the ideal, and that the final culmination of it in the abolition of war and the complete organization of the world on a basis of goodwill, friendly co-operation, and the peaceful arbitration of all controversies is to be expected in the near future.[8]

The classic *Encyclopaedia of Religion and Ethics,* edited by James Hastings, contains an essay by Professor R. L. Ottley of Oxford. Published just before World War I would blow away the lives of his students, the essay by the good divine concluded:

> While war itself in the modern world has been more and more completely brought under the control of international law, it has also yielded in a measure to the practice of arbitration. In this region also the Christian spirit is a force that makes for international unity and control.[9]

The content of his essay is basically that while *shalom* of the Old Testament is a vision, in the New Testament peace is realized. Peace is bound up with Jesus' victory, it is a gift of God, it is a blessing for the individual soul, and it is basically irrelevant to issues of international war. Christians as peaceful, restrained people contribute a peaceful spirit as this is seen in his generally utopian perspective on the world on the brink of destruction.

One reads these essays written after nineteen hundred years of Christian faith with a bitter sadness that the faith had produced so little wisdom. It also cautions us to be careful in our presumption of knowledge. There is no guarantee that we can read our times and God's will any better than those two foolish Christian scholars read their time.

In its most frequent usage in the Old Testament, "Shalom is an emphatically social concept."[10] It has a very broad range of meanings; it has a certain imprecision in particular usages. Basically it means "well-being." It points to national prosperity. As a personal greeting it is a wish for bodily health. Between peoples it implies an alliance, a relationship; it has covenanted implications. Solomon and Hiram (I Kings 5:12) have *shalom* in an alliance. The covenant of God with Israel is a covenant of peace (Isaiah 54:10). In its full meaning, *shalom* is a religious term because it is a gift of God. *Shalom* is often one of other expected elements of eschatological fulfillment (Zechariah 9:10).

In the prophets *shalom* refers to a "real political peace for Israel." The false prophets prophesied such a real peace when it was not to be realized. Jeremiah and Ezekiel pleaded for Israel to see that its real future in the immediate future was war and destruction (Ezekiel 13:16). *Shalom* can be translated as salvation and the Old Testament scholar von Rad says that the translator of *shalom* is often at a loss over how to express it exactly.[11]

The New Testament, through its dependence on the Greek translation of the Hebrew Bible, brings the meaning of "well-being" of *shalom* into Greek, displacing the more passive Greek meaning of "eirene" or being at a state of rest. Both *shalom* and *eirene* have the meaning of peace as opposed to war. This is the fundamental meaning of peace in the realist approach to international issues. Peace does mean well-being, even salvation. It means being with God, particularly in the New Testament. It is used in greetings in both rabbinical literature and in the New Testament to wish well-being. In the New Testament usages, various layers of meaning can be found including, (1) peace as a feeling of rest, (2) peace as reconciliation, (3) peace as salvation, and (4) peace as salvatory relations among people.[12]

Matthew 5:9, "Blessed are the peacemakers, for they shall be called sons of God," is the only use of *peacemaker* in the New Testament. "The reference is to those who disinterestedly come between two contending parties and try to make peace. These God calls his sons because they are like Him."[13] Here, as in other Greek literature, we have peace used as the opposite of war. Sometimes the peacemaker is the ruler who establishes peace in the world.[14] Matthew's blessing may be eschatological but it recommends an active role of promoting peace. It is stronger than Paul's recommendation in his list of moral teachings to the Romans in Romans 12:18: "If possible, so far as it depends upon you, live peaceably with all."

Shalom or *eirene* meaning salvation are at the center of the Christian faith. They are more than vision: Personally and in community they may be realized. Socially and politically they are not realized, but in both Old Testament and New Testament the faithful are urged to live peaceably, to be peacemakers.

There is no credible way to imply that ancient writers knew anything at all about the possibilities of humanity ultimately destroying itself. Confronted as we are, however, with the question of whether or not human beings will survive, the meaning of peacemaking for our time involves the salvation of humanity as a species. Peacemaking and promoting peace may go on in the family, in school, in business, in church, and in government. But in most cases these are not ultimate questions of being. Theologically speaking, peacemaking today means the practical, activist work in society to prevent the destruction of the human species. Its primary focus is preventing global nuclear war. The further meaning of peacemaking is developed by inquiring into the origins of war.

The Origins of War

Human history is filled with war. No people have been free of conflict for very long. The epics of Western civilization, whether the Greek *Iliad* or the Hebrew Bible, point to the story of history and myth as one of renewed warfare. We know of peace as a longed-for time of dreaming and innocence, a time before civilization. We know of it as a promise for the future, the time of restoration of innocence, but actual history is filled with the noise of battle.

War is fascinating and frightening. Humanity is both drawn into its vortex and appalled by its horror. In such a recognition the attractive power of war is seen. War participates to a significant degree in the description that Rudolph Otto applied to the holy. The experience of the holy is awesome in its attractiveness and in its dread. In the *Idea of the Holy*, the meaning of the holy is found partially in the feelings of a fearful awe and in fascination. As Christians we tend to be so comforted by trust in grace that we forget the judgment of the ultimate. Fear is somehow foreign to us. Yet this ambiguity of the divine confronts us in the phenomenon of war. We can be fascinated by movies showing the destruction of the earth or even the Star Wars movies of the destruction of worlds beyond our nuclear-wrecked earth, yet we know that the threat of massive war will obliterate all our meanings.

Our ancient sources of wisdom, whether they be Hindu, Hebrew, or Hellene, see war as the work of gods. People do not really decide for war, they are pawns of the spiritual forces that in their own contradictions cause humanity to fight. In our present state of Christian monotheism, which emphasizes that freedom is necessary if humanity is to fulfill its purpose of loving God, we cannot blame the gods for our wars. Yet, we are wise to recognize the reality of the forces of human spiritual principalities and powers, which flow through us individually and communally and drive us toward war. In the *Iliad*, the Old Testament, and the *Bhagavad Gita*, the responsibility of the gods for war should certainly teach even the most rational among us to recognize what the ancients knew: War is a problem of our existence.

It is not just a political problem; it is a problem of our spiritual-political life. It is a problem of our species and of its organization.

In a brilliant analysis of the history of the philosophy of war, Kenneth Waltz finds three major explanations for the origin of war in the history of Western thought.[15] The first explanation of war is that humanity is flawed. Whether the major cause be ignorance, pride, greed, or alienation, the problem is in human nature. The second explanation is that the nation-states are organized to pursue war. Whether the wars be owing to economic self-interest, national pride, national insecurity, the political pressures of the masses, or the structural place of the military in the country, wars are basically owing to the follies of nations in their organization and policies. Finally, there are those thinkers who place the origins of war in international anarchy. As long as there is no sovereign to enforce order, autonomous units of the international system will resort to armed conflict to resolve their inevitable tensions. Whether the tensions are the result of economic competition, exaggerated nationalism, border disputes, or ideological disputes, it is the international anarchy that permits war. Waltz's *Man, the State and War* provides a necessary perspective on the complexity of the causes of war. Obviously none of the factors that have been identified as primary sources of war can be excluded. The Christian who fully realizes that we are living in a season of "war and rumors of war" appreciates all three sources of war: international anarchy, war-structured states, and the foibles of human nature.

The use of this stylized presentation of Western thought about the origins of war as a principle of interpretation permits us to discover the same patterns in the eighth-century B.C. prophet Isaiah of Jerusalem. Isaiah forged the motto of the United Nations:

> They shall beat their swords into ploughshares,
> and their spears into pruning hooks. (Isaiah 2:4*b*)

The vision of peace is of course a vision of a transformed humanity, nation, and international order. It is not the task of the political rulers of Jerusalem to accomplish; it is an eschatological vision of hope. Underneath the eschatological vision, in the first three chapters of Isaiah, is Isaiah's critique of Judah revealing the origins of war. The vision itself, verses 1-4 of chapter 2, contains the structure of international order replacing anarchy. "All the nations" are brought to the teaching of God's ways. An international community is founded on accepted teachings and accepted ways of life. There is also common judgment and the recognition of a common sovereign.

> He shall judge between the nations,
>   and shall decide for many peoples. (Isaiah 2:4a)

After the common sovereignty and practice are accepted, disarmament follows:

> And they shall beat their swords into ploughshares,
>   and their spears into pruning hooks.

Finally, after disarmament, or more profoundly, after the conversion of weapons into agricultural tools, the nations abandon teaching and planning for war:

> nation shall not lift up sword against nation,
>   neither shall they learn war any more.

Here in the vision, elements of international sovereignty, accepted teaching, agreed-upon patterns of life, and common judgment proceed disarmament and the abandonment of war. All those who stress that the origins of war lie in anarchy should be encouraged by this wisdom. Certainly the Isaiah text is a fit motto, though visionary, for a United Nations which was born amid hopes of abridging international anarchy.

However, in turning to the chapters of Isaiah surrounding the vision, we find the reasons for the wars that were to destroy Jerusalem. The nation is described as a "sinful nation." It has rebelled against the Lord in specific, identifiable ways: Justice has been corrupted (1:4), there is "no soundness in it" (1:6), the worship of the people has not been accompanied by justice but by violence, so the religious life is corrupted and rejected by God (1:14-15), the rulers associate with criminals (1:23), the weak are not defended (1:23). Jerusalem is given a chance to escape war through repentance, but the nation would have to become just. The very wealth and pride of the nation is seen as an evil leading to idolatry (2:7-8). The critique that promises war as punishment is against the pride of the nation and particularly against its armament program (2:15-16). Our stylized principle of interpretation confronts a difficulty in the reality of the text. It is impossible to know precisely whether the condemnation of the elders of Jerusalem for preventing justice belongs more appropriately to the corruption of the nation or to the failings of individuals, but the expression is so general that it can be included under the failure of the nation.

> The Lord enters into judgment
>   with the elders and princes of his people:
> "It is you who have devoured the vineyard,
>   the spoil of the poor is in your houses.
> What do you mean by crushing my people,
>   by grinding the face of the poor?"
> says the Lord God of hosts. (Isaiah 3:14-15)

These texts certainly assume that the punishment of war falls on corrupted states, which neglect justice. In the lack of soundness of nation, in pride and exploitation, there can be no peace. We can say either there is no peace without justice or that peace includes justice. We are not entitled to conclude that relative justice in the nation ensures peace, because the nation still in history is a unit in anarchy, which can be led into war by broken leaders. The text presupposes that the world is such that war destroys the unjust. The picture is of God actively calling the enemy army to invade from afar (Isaiah 5:26-30). We know of many cases in the last few years in which national injustices led to war. A theology that followed Reinhold Niebuhr would probably trace out the many historical causes that led from injustice to war while proclaiming the just God as the meaning and fulfillment of history. A theology following Alfred North Whitehead would see God, as the structure of value of the universe, producing war when humans pursue injustice in the conditions of international instability. Liberation theologians with some reference to Marxist-Leninist theories of the wars of imperialism can see how the exploitation of the poor by the wealthy leads to war. In each of the four cases, whether it be the simple action of God presupposed by Hebrew scripture or the more modern translations of that faith in terms of human freedom, national corruption brings war.

Finally, the text teaches individual human responsibility for war. Human beings as persons are corrupted and their actions bring war. The political leaders accept bribes, corruption reigns; they seek gifts, and do not administer justice (1:23). The judges and the counselors have fallen away (1:26). Individuals as well as the community have rebelled and forgotten God's purposes (1:2-3). The hands of the people are unfit to worship as "your hands are full of blood" (1:15). Isaiah's description of the evils of Jerusalem remind the reader of the realistic descriptions by Machiavelli in sixteenth-century Italy or Hobbes in seventeenth-century England. It is hard to know exactly the chief expression of human failing in Isaiah since the text is so synthetically rich and not explicitly analytical. An analysis founded on the perspective of Reinhold Niebuhr would tend to emphasize the critique of pride, which is so explicitly emphasized. Here the pride of the male rulers is complemented by the haughtiness of the rich women of Zion. The women are not blamed for misrule, but for prideful conspicuous consumption (1:16). Pride is usually regarded as more basic to sin than greed in Niebuhr's analysis. The liberation theology would tend not to emphasize the pride as much as the consumption and could focus on the fifth chapter, which condemns the displacement of the small farmer from his land. The Whiteheadian perspective would see the disruption by way of breaking the harmony and violating the unity. The ignorance of the knowledge of reality would also be highlighted:

> The ox *knows* its owner,
>   and the ass its master's crib;
> but Israel does not know,
>   my people does not understand. (1:3, emphasis mine)

The first three chapters are illuminated by Waltz's categories, but in a very powerful way, the fifth chapter of Isaiah exhibits a cause of war that needs for our day to be highlighted. It reflects all three prior motifs—the weakness of persons because of human alienation, the corruption of the state, and international disorder—but the focus is on the displacement of the peasant from the land.

In the eighth century B.C. in Judah, the plight of the majority of the rural population worsened. It was a time of expanded military and economic power for both Israel and Judah. The powers of the ruling elites were increased and the peasant land holdings were reduced. The larger estates tended to produce olives, grapes, and grain for export. The exports helped finance the urban luxuries and the armies of the centralized state. As a consequence the deprivation of the peasantry increased and the eighth-century prophetic oracles addressed this issue.

The prophetic oracle in Isaiah 5 predicts two consequences. The large estates will be overthrown and the country desolated. Foreign armies will invade and ravage the land. Peacemakers need to meditate on these beautiful but devastating oracles to understand the present. They reinforce the liberation theology message that depriving the poor farmer from the land (whether it is Israeli deprivation of Palestinians, or Central American elite deprivation of peasants, or Indian landowners' deprivation of the rural workers of India) leads to social failure and to war.

The oracles of Isaiah 5 portray Israel as God's vineyard, which the Lord lovingly tended. But God's own vineyard did not produce. God looked for justice and saw violence. The powerful expanded their fields and deprived the poor and the result was disaster. In a study of comparative sociology's relevance to these oracles, D. N. Premnath of Bangalore, India, has focused on Isaiah 5:8-10.[16]

> Woe to those who join house to house,
>   who add field to field,
> until there is no more room,
>   and you are made to dwell alone
>   in the midst of the land.
>
> The Lord of hosts has sworn in my hearing:
> "Surely many houses shall be desolate,
>   large and beautiful houses without inhabitant.
> For ten acres of vineyard shall yield
>   but one bath,
>   and a homer of seed shall yield
>   but an ephah."

This impoverishing of the rural population, which the oracle condemns and which contains within it the promise of conflict, is real in India today. The poverty of the rural class continues and by some measures worsens. Fifty percent of the rural population is without land. Fifty percent of the national population cannot afford one square meal a day. As a result, violence bubbles in the population just below the repression. Liberals in the Western world know the truth of the problem when they preach land reform. But their practice belies their preaching. The Alliance for Progress promised land reform for Latin America at a time when even in North America the poorer agricultural population was being displaced from its land. In the 1980s land reform is promised in Central America, but its administration in the hands of the American allied elite dooms it to frustration. The problem is not just one of North American greed, though, or capitalism. State socialism has shown the same tendency to displace the peasants from their land. In Stalin's Ukraine, millions starved to death under the forced collectivizing and usurping of agricultural produce for the urban population. Out of this horror, sectors of the population were ready to welcome even Hitler's liberation until they discovered the invaders to be worse than the Russian oppressors. Hebrew nobility, Indian landowners, North American capitalists, and Stalinist socialists all sow havoc as they take the land. These prophetic oracles of the eighth century B.C. provide a valuable insight into the origins of human conflict and the causes of war.[17] The outcome of the oracle was that the large landowners too shall be displaced, their beautiful houses left empty. Finally, after listing the evils of Israel and Judah, the fifth chapter concludes with war. A terrible army is to come that cannot be resisted:

> Their roaring is like a lion
>   like young lions they roar;
> they growl and seize their prey,
>   they carry it off, and none can rescue. (Isaiah 5:29)

From Waltz's twentieth-century book and the first chapters of Isaiah's eight-century B.C. book, the multifaceted origins of war are seen. If war's scourge falls on us because of the weakness of human nature, the inadequacy of our nation-states, the anarchy of our international order, and our human greed displacing the people from the land, can we avoid it? Can we be both realistic about the persistent tendencies toward war and affirmative of the centrality of peacemaking to the Christian faith? As a Marxist philosopher engaged in seeking peace asked me in a meeting in Prague, "Does Christian faith show a way through the danger of war?"

II. CHRISTIAN REALISM AND PEACEMAKING

Christian realism tends to treat problems of social philosophy and social action from the perspective of an alienated humanity locked in struggle. In trying to achieve more social cooperation, we must not neglect the social struggle. The realists all tend to emphasize both morality and the difficulties of applying morality to political reality. Social strategies tend to be derived from the historical context of a given issue. Morality tends to be derived not from the social situation, but from the articulated moral tradition. The morality of a given social strategy depends in realist perspective on the prudent match between moral tradition and social situation. Realists castigate as idealists those who they believe have not allowed sufficiently for the social situation and as cynics those who ignore the moral tradition. So the Christian realists reject both Thomas More's *Utopia* and Niccolò Machiavelli's *The Prince* as models of political ethics. They tend to approve of Augustine's political ethics from *The City of God* and John Calvin's political thought in *The Institutes of the Christian Religion*.[1]

The realism relevant to this study is in the North American form shaped by the ethicist Reinhold Niebuhr, by the political philosopher of international relations Hans J. Morgenthau, and by the historian of U.S.-Soviet relations George Kennan. The younger generation of realists divides around issues of perception of the cold war, human rights, the just-war tradition, and domestic politics. But in the three names mentioned there is an identifiable consensus and an approach to international relations. These central thinkers of Christian realism were all non-Marxist in their methodology. They were all more oriented to reflection upon international relations by means of historical reflection than by systematic models. All were interested in the practice of U.S. foreign policy as well as its theory. They tended to view the relationship with the Soviet Union as competitive but argued for cooperation in meeting the threats of nuclear war. They tended to prefer pragmatic, melioristic approaches rather than utopian approaches. They tended to work from within their inherited traditions rather than spurning their past and looking for a new tradition. An important example of their acceptance of tradition is their recognition of the Christ-Caesar synthesis of Constantine.

Christ and Caesar

Almost twenty centuries ago there were rivals to the title The Prince of Peace. Romans celebrating the end of the civil wars that had wreaked so much havoc proclaimed their emperor Augustus the Prince of Peace. Christians drawing on the prophecy of Isaiah regarded Jesus the Prince of Peace. Luke precedes his mention of Augustus with the reference to Zechariah's prophecy, including:

> For in the tender compassion of our God
>   the morning sun from heaven will rise upon us,
> to shine on those who live in darkness, under
>   the cloud of death,
>   and to guide our feet into
> the way of peace. (Luke 1:78-79 NEB)

Augustus may be regarded as the symbol of peace through military force. He defeated his rivals and imposed a Roman peace, an achievement not to be underrated. Jesus was the announcer of a different way; he was the proclaimer of the reign of God. His way to peace was (and is) through forgiveness, humility, and love. Violence surrounded Jesus from his birth to his death. The defenders of Augustus' peace finally crucified him.

However, the servants of Rome and the servants of Jesus, both pursuing peace, continued to struggle. Inflamed by the power of the resurrected Christ, the church persisted, though persecuted. In its persistence it refused for decades to sanction military service, though Jesus himself never specifically condemned it. It testified to a new way of community through reconciliation and kept its mind focused on God's peace while avoiding disturbing earthly peace. This peaceable community proved more attractive than the Roman peace, which continually broke down into fratricidal wars. Eventually, in the midst of one of these civil wars, which had proved how fragile Roman peace really was, a candidate for the imperial chair saw a vision. Constantine began a pilgrimage that eventually led to his baptism and to uniting the empire around the worship of God through Christ. Though this synthesis was not strong enough to preserve Rome, it preserved the new Rome in Constantinople until the fifteenth century. Christians gave up their reluctance, in the main, to use military force, though they often shielded clerics and monks from military force and tried to tame warfare.

So by the fourth century the future emperor defeated his rival under the sign of the Christ (☧). History had contrived a synthesis, an unstable union perhaps, but still a synthesis that was sanctified by the emperor's presiding over the theological conclave, the Council of Nicea, and attempting to require theological unity within his empire.

The faith that had undermined the empire was now translated into the civil religion. Some Christians have regarded this as a great apostasy. Many Roman pagans also decried the new synthesis and tried to destroy it. Most Christians since Augustine however, have accepted the synthesis and tried to make it work. It became the social reality of the Western world.

Today, we still feel the tensions of that synthesis. Washington, D.C., the capital of the Western alliance, conducts its affairs from buildings sporting neo-Classical architecture. It operates without an emperor, but a senate helps shape foreign policy, and Washington worries over imperial presidencies. Its single largest religious community calls itself Roman Catholicism, and its other predominant religious bodies reflect their origins in Roman Catholicism while hearkening back for their distinctiveness to scripture written in the Roman Empire.

Like those in Zechariah's day (Luke 1:79), we live in darkness under a cloud of death. Death has always been a threat, but today the cloud of death is particularly real as preparation for a final war runs ahead, seemingly out of control. We live in an armed truce under a reign of nuclear terror that threatens to destroy the world. Can the synthesis of Jesus' peacemaking and Augustus' peacemaking be made to work? How do we relate the love of Jesus to the world of practical power today? Obviously, a relationship of love to power for the sake of peace today cannot be attempted in an exclusively Christian way. It can be attempted in ways consistent with and dependent on Christian faith, but it must also acknowledge the search for peace in the world's great religions and parareligious traditions. The goal is peace for the world, not just for the Western world, which is itself religiously and politically pluralistic.

There are many who would separate realism and peacemaking. It is easier to attempt to discuss world politics without regard for the longing for peace. Alternatively there is a temptation to define peace in other-worldly or purely individual terms and to deny the relevance of contemporary problems. Nonreligious people may want to exclude faith from the perspective with which they view pressing world problems. Religious people can easily articulate philosophies that give up on the world and settle for only an individual or heavenly peace. Wise people can nod to either peacemaking or realism, but emphasize their primary concern so that the other factor is relegated to minor consideration. Realism without a primary concern for peacemaking, however, degenerates into *realpolitik* and into destructive cynicism. Peacemaking without due acknowledgment of the reality of the forces that resist peace falls into illusions that do not deserve to be taken seriously on a threatened planet. The two concerns must be united. A test case for Christians trying to unite the search for peace and the reality of the twentieth century has been the cold war.

Christian Realism and the Cold War

Reinhold Niebuhr (1892–1971) was the most important recent Protestant theologian on issues of international relations and his thought has had tremendous effect on statesmen in the United States and abroad. In the 1940s and 1950s he was regarded as one who spoke out against communism and helped prepare the United States to assume responsibilities of empire and cold war. When I came to know him, though, in the 1960s, he was opposing the war in Vietnam, rejecting militant cold war rhetoric, and pleading for a recognition of the U.S.-Soviet partnership in managing the nuclear danger. A new look into his thought can help us toward a perspective on peacemaking and realism.

Niebuhr's many debates with Christian pacifists and his polemics against idealists in politics have obscured his commitment to the search for peace. His fate is not too different from that of Hans Morgenthau, whose passion for peace is seen in the title of his famous text, *Politics Among Nations: The Struggle for Power and Peace.*[2] Power was central to international politics for both Niebuhr and Morgenthau, but their goal was peace. Because both identified themselves as realists it has been hard even for some students of policy to accept that both opposed vigorously the United States' recent, horrible war in Vietnam. The other direct use of U.S. military force abroad during Niebuhr's later years was President Johnson's intervention in the Dominican Republic, and Niebuhr opposed that in print also.[3]

Still, the major critique of Niebuhr's public policy positions resides in his thought regarding the cold war. Probably only consistent pacifists would decry his support of the United States' participation in World Wars I and II. Opinion divides around the support for the United States' position in the Korean War. Only hard-line anti-Communists would vigorously criticize Niebuhr for his critique of U.S. policy in Vietnam. Walter LaFeber regards Niebuhr as one of the main systematic thinkers who contributed to the philosophy of the American cold war warriors. His *America, Russia and the Cold War* attributes immense influence to Niebuhr in shaping American thinking about the cold war.

A fellow theologian has put the point sharply. John M. Swomley accuses Niebuhr of providing "the religious rationale for the military foreign policy that created the contemporary American empire and the policy of global intervention culminating in the war in Vietnam."[4] Building on the insight of Charles West, he suggests that Christian realism served an ideological role in justifying American empire.

The record shows that Niebuhr did consciously provide rationale for competition with the Soviet Union while he explicitly attacked U.S. policy in Vietnam. One of his most famous essays, "The King's Chapel and the King's Court," explicitly attacked the attempt by the Nixon administration to legitimate religiously its policies in Vietnam and at home.[5]

He had hoped during World War II for postwar cooperation among the allies, but tensions between the Soviet Union and the Western allies convinced him during the war that both sides would try to advance their own interests. The collapse of the wartime alliance led him to regard the Soviet Union as a dangerous opponent. Its creed and policies led him to believe that it was important to rally the United States to assume responsibility after the war and to oppose the presumed ambitions of the Soviet Union. The role of Niebuhr in leading American liberals to oppose Communism is well known. As he had provided arguments for opposing Nazism before and during World War II, he supported opposing Communism.

He perceived that maintaining competitive existence between the United States and the Soviet Union was necessary to maintaining peace. "There cannot be war between us without mutual annihilation. There must not be war."[6] He envisaged the competition extending for decades or even longer. There could be no resolution through war, but neither partner in the competition could be expected to surrender its respective myths or ideologies. Wise statesmanship was the most important element in maintaining the uneasy partnership in preventing nuclear war. He had no great confidence in education, cultural exchanges, religious impulses, or disarmament plans eliminating the tension caused by the two continental empires competing for influence and interests in the world. This view of the world, essentially of two nuclear-armed scorpions locked in a small bottle, was not a world he would have wished for, but it was the world he perceived. It was also a world subjected to the winds of revolutionary demands flowing through the developing world, and a world made more dangerous and unified by technological development.

He warned of the danger of the United States' overreliance on military power. The tendency to build defense pacts in Asia revealed little understanding of the political complexities there. Military force could be effective in crises, but without political forces of cohesion, military force could accomplish little as demonstrated in both Vietnam and China. Overreliance on military power was a temptation to a nation as wealthy as the United States, but it could contribute to our political embarrassment. Military force for Niebuhr was a last resort, but the American temptation was to use it as a meat-ax where subtlety was called for. The understanding of the needs of a population required wise statecraft, not primarily military power.[7]

The real task of preserving the nuclear stalemate rested in the political sphere. He noted that technical miscalculation might bring about the nuclear catastrophe, but his primary concern was in political miscalculation. A defeat in some vital area of competition he reasoned might tempt one side or the other in hysteria to resort to nuclear weapons. This I think was the central reason for his continued reference to the "balance of power" in the post–World War II situation. He often described it as a "nuclear umbrella"; competition could go on, but it must be limited so as not to threaten the vital interests of the other party. Of course, it was not balance of power in any prenuclear meaning of the term, but an arrangement, ironically stumbled into, which was now securing not peace in any deep sense, but at least the avoidance of the nuclear holocaust.

He rejected the notion of "winning the cold war," and I do not think he ever entertained the idea of "rolling back Communism" as John Foster Dulles had dreamed of briefly. Without war and without hysteria, he counseled the United States to meet the Soviet challenge. "World peace required that the dynamic of this strange political movement be contained, its ambition to control the world be frustrated, and its revolutionary ardors be tamed by firm and patient resistance."[8]

Niebuhr regarded the complex and threatening postwar world as requiring "shrewder calculations of both ideological and power factors than we are accustomed to give them."[9] One of the questions is, how shrewd was Reinhold Niebuhr? Was he just commenting on the world in countless editorials, articles, and numerous books on empire, power, and American history? Or was he trying to have a political effect? I think he was being very political in his writing. In a major essay on the theory of international politics he wrote, "If power is identical with authority, it follows that the climate of a culture or its 'ideology,' which sanctions a particular type of authority, is really the ultimate source of power."[10]

Niebuhr knew that the facts did not interpret themselves. The complexities of the international world had to be reduced to be graspable, and put into perspective to become politically relevant. Niebuhr did not write much about method in either theology or international politics. But what he wrote about myth, symbol, and ideology reveals that he knew that in the articulation of myth, symbol, or ideology resided power. The expression of the myth was itself a creative act even as it remained loyal, to the best of one's ability, to the materials being discussed. Millions of events were taking place in the world but he would write, "Thus modern history is fated to be governed by the contrasting myths of the two super powers."[11] He knew that these myths were not easily changed and that he was powerless to affect the mythology or perspective of the Soviet Union. He did however set out to affect the mythology of the United States and to affect the perspective of the United States in its understanding of the Soviet Union. So his critics who accuse him of presenting an ideology for the United States' participation in the cold war are correct. The perspective he presented however was one of a precarious partnership between the United States and the Soviet Union in preserving a nuclear peace while struggling elsewhere. The struggle Niebuhr envisaged was primarily ideological since the contemporary source of authority for governance was less traditional and less religious than it had been in premodern society. Finally, authority rested on a governing group's ability not only to ensure order but also to deliver or promise a tolerably just society.

In the ideological struggle he felt that the United States with its ties to formerly colonial powers and its own problems of race and social injustice was at a temporary disadvantage in the developing world. However the creed and actual accomplishments of Communism were so badly flawed that he believed patient resistance would eventually encourage other governments to find their own solutions without succumbing to alliances with Communist powers.

Technological aid and economic aid were among the major contributions the United States could make to the health of the developing nations. In 1962 he would regard the ability of a democratic process to provide funds for aid as "the litmus test of the capacity of a democracy to survive in the contest."[12] The transfer of funds and knowledge to the developing nations still remains in the late twentieth century one of the crucial issues of the health of the world system.

Elsewhere, I have criticized Niebuhr's overly optimistic expectations for the Alliance for Progress.[13] It is unfortunate though that his critic John M. Swomley, Jr., takes part of the paragraph in which he is arguing for a strong interventionist policy in Latin America in the terms of the Alliance for Progress as evidence of Niebuhr's advocacy of imperial self-interest and neglects to mention that his use of economic power was for attempted land reform and education.[14] For the sake of changes in the oligarchic practices of Latin America, he urged intervention that would override liberal reservations about anti-imperialism. To Niebuhr, the United States was an empire in a struggle. Critics often seem to find fault with Niebuhr as if he were responsible either for the empire or the struggle. Certainly his views shaped our perspectives on the empire and the struggles, but they are rooted in reality as well as perspective. A sympathetic reading of Reinhold Niebuhr's writing finds him urging a cautious policy of statecraft, the building up of the developing world, a nuclear partnership, a decrease in American reliance on military power, outright rejection of United States policy in Vietnam, and a struggle to criticize and replace political leadership responsible for it.

Competitive coexistence in Niebuhr's perspective called for ideological debate. So while he tried to clarify and reform American ideology by interpreting its religious and secular elements, he criticized the pretensions and illusions of Marxism severely. This very criticism of Marxism can be seen as fueling the cold war. In Niebuhr's perspective, however, it was exactly the ideological debate that needed to be carried on and the United States needed to follow Senator Fulbright's idea of not trying "to redress ideological deficiencies with military power."[15] He feared the dominance of the military-industrial complex, criticized its dominance of the U.S. economy, and resisted journalistically some of its demands for new systems.[16]

Doves in the peace movement will probably never be at ease with Niebuhr. He had been president of the pacifist organization Fellowship of Reconciliation, and editor of the pacifist newspaper *The World Tomorrow*. His resignation from the F.O.R., in the Depression, had been over the possibility of sanctioning the use of violence by the workers in defense against capitalist owners in American industrial strife. His pacifism proved to be a pragmatic preference for nonviolent means of social change, but it could not be absolutist. Eventually, with Augustine he came to believe that the peace of the world was defended by violence or the threat of violence. So in 1948 he joined the debate over U.S. foreign policy with an article in *Life* entitled "For Peace We Must Risk War." Statecraft would seek to broaden national interest and attempt to reconcile the two, but force remained a last resort.

Hawks could never be content with Niebuhr either. Even in World War II he argued against the policy of unconditional surrender, attacked the policies of massive bombing of German cities, sponsored German refugees and German political groups in the United States working for moderation in the treatment of Germany, and helped defeat the Morgenthau plan for reducing postwar Germany to a pastoral economy. With Augustine, he believed peace to be among the highest achievements, but that to preserve it required a mixture of means including political authority, which relied both on agreement and force.

On questions of disarmament, then, he was not a dreamer. He had lived through a history of difficulty with disarmament plans in the early twentieth century. The ban on nuclear testing in the atmosphere he regarded as a great achievement and he thought the negotiations to stop the antiballistic missile race were a gain. The nonproliferation treaty seemed to him of dubious worth because it represented the satiation of the "haves" and the repression of the "have-nots."[17] Community had to precede disarmament or at least accompany it in its formation. The formation of that community was significantly begun in the work of the United Nations Economic and Social Council (UNESCO), in which he served as a U.S. delegate, but finally it required the moderation of the revolutionary ardor of Communism, the development of the Third World, and wise statecraft on the part of the Atlantic Alliance. So there was no guarantee of peace.

The building of community as seen in the work of UNESCO was of course flawed. The flaws revealed the spiritual nature of contemporary humanity. Modern humanity had to find ways of continuing to build community across international borders and of avoiding discouragement when it failed to complete the tasks. His comment on UNESCO stands as his attitude toward the building of world community.

> Here is an organization which seeks to realize the impossible: a world community. It must not regard this end as a simple possibility; but neither can it dismiss the task as an impossibility. It stands, therefore, constantly at the final limit of the human situation where the possible and the impossible are curiously intermingled and where it is difficult to distinguish between God's and our possibilities.[18]

The difference between Niebuhr and the neoconservative hawks of the Reagan administration can be seen in his realistic hopes for UNESCO; his theological hope was complemented by his personal work for UNESCO. The Reagan administration has withdrawn from UNESCO because its work became "too political" and too unappreciative of American perspectives.

UNESCO, of course, could not create world community. It could foster cultural exchanges, the spread of ideas across international borders, and the improvement of education. Education as we know it seems not to make people any more peace-loving. The sharing of the heights of another's culture has done little to promote peace among European nations, who for centuries have enjoyed one another's cultural creations. One could have hope for UNESCO's work, one could even believe the intellectual case for a world government to solve the world's insecurity was unassailable, and still not see a way to an international community tending toward the creation of a world government.

International agencies, laws, and trade mutually moved toward greater international integration and toward greater national interdependence. The spread of arms through trade and the development of national industries reinforced the driving tendency of decolonization to create more independent centers of national power. Niebuhr's friend Hans Morgenthau argued more fervently for the desirability of a world government than did Niebuhr, but neither could see a way to approach it.

Morgenthau's *magnum opus, Politics Among Nations,* eloquently analyzes the possibilities of different peace strategies. Peace is the central issue of the study of international relations. "Two world wars within a generation and the potentialities of nuclear warfare have made the establishment of international order and the preservation of international peace the paramount concern of Western civilization."[19]

Yet as the struggle for power characterizes the rivalry of the Soviet Union and the United States, peace through armament, disarmament, or world government seems unlikely. The more likely approach to peace in the superpower rivalry is through understanding, defining purposes, and negotiating conflicts.

The realistic perspective on the Soviet Union implies the need for three developments. (1) The United States must quickly learn more about the Soviet Union. This knowledge is needed by the public to support wise foreign policy. It is also needed at the highest levels of government to permit the formulation of prudent policy. (2) The most that can be expected is melioristic improvements in relations with the Soviet Union. Even in the climate of a Gorbachev leading in democratic and humanitarian directions, the traditional mores of Russia and of Russian communism will continue to exert their controlling influences. (3) The United States needs to turn more toward the art of diplomacy and accommodating differences.

The emphasis on the hopes of Jesus for peace and his own nonviolence receive such a great emphasis in the peace movement that a text in which he reflects on prudent realism needs to be treasured today:

> Or what king, going to encounter another king in war, will not sit down first and take counsel whether he is able with ten thousand to meet him

who comes against him with twenty thousand? And if not, while the other is yet a great way off, he sends an embassy and asks terms of peace? (Luke 14:31-32)

Like Reinhold Niebuhr, Hans Morgenthau knew there would be no world peace without a world government. World government is impossible without a lot more world community than is on the horizon. He concluded his philosophy of international politics with the necessity of achieving peace through diplomatic accommodation. World community can be built best through diplomatic accommodation, and it is necessary to have revitalized diplomacy now to secure what peace is possible and to prevent nuclear war.

A revitalized diplomacy would be one divested of crusading spirits so that competing national interests could be compromised. The goals of foreign policy would be defined carefully according to the limits of real interests and available power. The perspectives of other nations would always be considered and the needs for compromises protecting those perspectives recognized.

A revitalized diplomacy recognizing that· peace between the superpowers is the *sine qua non* of diplomacy would not hold to abstract prerogatives of legal right at the sacrifice of political wisdom. It would be careful about claiming positions it cannot hold, and it would avoid strong commitments to weak allies. Diplomacy must subject the armed forces to the procedures of politics and not allow the military to set the political stage. The government of a republic must lead political opinion within the ethos of a country so that its policies are not disrupted by shortsighted passions, particularly those clamoring for conflict. A road to international peace through an accommodating diplomacy is not a romantic road, but the realists tend to regard it as the best opportunity.[20]

Diplomacy is guided by political interest. Two powerful contemporary forces neglect political interests. Nationalism feeding on human inadequacies projects a fervor for the symbol of the nation, which overrides rational politics. Militarism neglects the political goals of the people for the sake of preparing for war. Preparation for war can launch forces that in themselves will cause wars no one could rationally desire.

George Kennan thinks that the forces of nationalism and militarism conspired to incline Europe toward World War I.[21] The developing belief in the nineteenth century of the inevitability of war reinforced the tendency to subvert national diplomacy to the needs of military planning, and European wars resulted. In the early twentieth century the forces of life on planet earth could restore life, and humanity could stand the carnage. But in the late twentieth century the control of nuclear physics makes human recovery from war unlikely. Nationalism and modern militarism can no longer be rationally cultivated. They must be curtailed.

Kennan more than Niebuhr or Morgenthau sees that the new weapons themselves have become the problem. There are conflicts of interests, the two societies are quite disparate, and the political scene in the world lacks order. The central problem however is the preparation of the two sides for war. War is not inevitable, but the military buildup and the gathering hostility between the Soviet Union and the United States increases its likelihood.

Kennan does not believe that the Soviet Union intends to attack either Western Europe or the United States. Consequently the major support for huge expenditures to deter such attacks is groundless. Neither the capacities nor the known intentions of the Soviets give adequate reason to expect such an attack. Moreover the history of the development of nuclear arms provides evidence that the Soviet Union usually responds to U.S. arms development. The increase on both sides of weapons of mass destruction lessens the security of people on both sides. The Reagan administration's abandoning of SALT II and the questioning of the 1972 Anti-Ballistic Missile Treaty are moves that decrease American security. Arms control agreements incorporating deep cuts in weapons of mass destruction are needed to break the momentum of a rush toward war. Other immediate priorities he repeatedly argues for include an agreement with the Soviet Union against first use of nuclear weapons, a comprehensive test ban treaty to stabilize the balance, and denuclearization of Northern and Central Europe.[22] Of course, Kennan is not recommending unilateral disarmament, nor is he against rational prudent strengthening of conventional armaments where appropriate.

Kennan's writing since 1950 on Soviet-U.S. relations is characterized by criticism of several aspects of Soviet society. He has not been an apologist for the Soviet Union. He tends to see the Soviet regime as saddled by a relatively stable and inflexible bureaucracy characterized by intrigue and fear of the West. He sees a people not highly motivated by the official ideology and plagued by inefficiency and rising alcoholism. His term as United States Ambassador to Moscow was abruptly ended when he was declared *persona non grata* for his critiques of Soviet society and of the isolation of diplomatic personnel in 1953.

Yet he believes that the Soviet pretensions to world domination of the early Russian communism have been abandoned. They cannot and do not intend to invade the West. Their loss of influence in China, Egypt, and Yugoslavia since the war outweigh the gains they have made elsewhere in the developing nations. They expand their influence as they can (as major powers traditionally do), but there is no threat to dominate the world.

They are determined to repress dissent in their Eastern European states and they will use armed force to accomplish it as necessary. Liberalizing puppet states in Eastern Europe awaits both guile on the part of Eastern Europeans, as demonstrated recently in Hungary, and possible internal changes in the Soviet Union. The victory of the hard-liners in the invasion of Afghanistan is certainly being proved a mistake. Kennan believes Brezhnev was unable to control the hard-liners in that issue and whether or not Gorbachev will completely extricate the army from that country remains to be seen. The world's criticism of that invasion was certainly in order, and the United States needed more support in opposing the Soviets there. It is a mistake, however, to use the condemned invasion of Afghanistan, a troubled border state with some of the same ethnic peoples as the Soviet Union, as an example of the first act of world conquest. For one hundred years Russians have meddled in Afghanistan; the British withdrawal east of Suez, the American failure in Iran, and Afghan Communist bungling provided a unique opportunity to the Soviet Union, which was seized.

Since 1949, Kennan has been urging the United States to a different view of the Soviet Union, incorporating less reliance on the threat of nuclear weapons. His failure to impress a moderate view of the Soviets on the foreign policy establishment has led him to see himself personally as an outsider. In a recent study of his thought, Barton Gellman tends to regard him as too pessimistic and almost cynical about American society.[23] Over against the optimism about American society of his young critic however, Kennan's record of a prophetic interpretation of the world danger and the corruption of American life seem true. Gellman fails to examine Kennan's Calvinistic spiritual roots. Kennan did not say much about his theological convictions in his early diplomatic writing. In his later writing, however, as the world situation has become more desperate, his references to theological critique have become more pronounced.

In 1982, Kennan delivered "A Christian's View of the Arms Race" at Princeton Theological Seminary; though he claimed no special erudition as a Christian theologian, he spoke out of his Christian conscience. He particularly emphasized the need to keep at a minimum the loss of civilian life in those rare instances in which a Christian might participate in war. Nuclear weapons offended against this principle. Probably, he thought, nuclear weapons should not even be considered a weapon like other weapons. But if so considered they were subject to the same rules of war as other weapons. Moreover these weapons were ruled invalid by Christian conscience. Nor could innocents be held hostage by governments for other governments' policies, as the theory of deterrence held.

His argument proceeds in line with Jonathan Schell's, that the threat to future generations is immoral. The threatened destruction of the "spiritual and intellectual achievements" of civilization is immoral. Humans could not take upon themselves the authority of planning to destroy the human framework, "which God meant . . . to proceed." He concluded his address:

> I cannot help it. I hope I am not being unjust or uncharitable. But to me, in the light of these considerations, the readiness to use nuclear weapons against other human beings—against people whom we do not know, whom we have never seen, and whose guilt or innocence it is not for us to establish—and, in doing so, to place in jeopardy the natural structure upon which all civilization rests, as though the safety and the perceived interests of our own generation were more important than everything that has ever taken place or could take place in civilization: this is nothing less than a presumption, a blasphemy, an indignity—an indignity of monstrous dimensions—offered to God![24]

This is where the Christian realist analysis comes out.[25] We must find another way to an appropriate international security. The quest returns us to Christian ethics of a fundamental order.

III. THE ETHICS OF PEACEMAKING

The quest of peacemaking in a warring world provides a trajectory for discussing Christian ethics. The direction of our action is toward peace. How can Christian ethics help in that movement? We are located in a particular history threatened in particular ways by the divisiveness of the political economy of the late twentieth century. Our religious tradition calls us toward a peace with justice, but the way is impeded by perceived restraints located in the human self, in our oppression of the poor, in our nations, and in our international disorder. The commitments already made incline us to find guidance within the center of Christian tradition related to public ethics.

There are many summaries of Christian theory, but the focus in this study on peacemaking ethics leads to the Pauline statement on the theory of Christian life:

> So faith, hope, love abide, these three; but the greatest of these is love.
> (I Corinthians 13:13)

These three virtues are essential. They may not contain all of Christian wisdom, but they summarize the transformative power of Christian virtue on humanity. If we were to desire a guide to Christian life we could do no better than Augustine did in using these three virtues as an outline. They serve as the three summarizing virtues of a theory of peacemaking. Here they are discussed in relation to the conflicts of the twentieth-century world.

Faith Not Idolatry

The first issue of life still remains faith vs. idolatry. The first commandment of Israel is: "I am the Lord your God, who brought you out of the land of Egypt, out of the house of bondage. You shall have no other gods before me" (Exodus 20:2-3). With Islam and Christianity, the polemic against idolatry is the first requirement of faith. In the Western world, we are inclined to think that idolatry has been overcome. A little examination of our cultures reveals their idolatrous character, however. Idolatry is the elevation of concerns that have relative value to the role of ultimate concern.

Experience in India in the midst of its many idols has freed me to appreciate more deeply the Hebrew polemic against idolatry and also to see its role in both North Atlantic countries and in Communist European countries. In India, idols are ubiquitous. They decorate the temples, they are beside the roads, they are in the museums, they are present at festivals and in parades. Their movements are described in the newspapers and the devotion to them has a social-political importance. The Hindu philosopher who escorted me through the Meenakshi Temple in Madurai directed his worship to the "One." His One had the characteristics of a Tillichian understanding of the ground of being. But he said that the people had no understanding. They basically worshiped the idols. This idolatry is woven into the national literature, the caste system, the subjection of women, the sanctity of cattle, the art, and the Hindu relativism. There are so many claims to ultimate reality that life, it seems, remains an illusion. One story is as good as another. Abuses of idolatry still involve sacralizing prostitution, human sacrifice, and the endorsement of fatalism. The resultant pluralism of an idolatrous polytheism psychologically reinforces tolerance of disorder, extreme communalism, and the relative neglect of a transforming ethic. All of this can easily drive Moslems and Christians into a fanatical rejection of Indian life, which when combined with imperial power has wrought terrible human destruction. India's internal disorder may render her less dangerous on the international scene because her resources are underdeveloped and fragmented.

The two most dangerous societies in the world are descended from the Hebrew polemic against idolatry. Neither the formerly Christian West nor the formerly Christian Eastern Europe suffer from the sort of idolatry that dominates India. Their secularization continues the anti-idolatry of the Hebrew prophets who smashed idols physically and with scorn. The secularization in the West has been inspired both by Protestant theism and enlightenment humanism. In the Communist world the motivation has been a militant atheism. Both societies officially operate secularly, and Christian minorities play roles of varying importance. It is really impossible to say whether the Christian minorities play a greater role in the Communist countries or in the mixed-economy democracies. Is the public role of the church, for example, greater in Canada or Poland? Is the church more vital in East or West Germany?

The idolatry of the Eastern European countries is state idolatry. The state has, in the name of an abandoned utopian revolution, assumed the economic role as well as the governance role. The role of the priests has been reduced and the commissar has assumed the roles of both the business leader and the political leader. This is evident to the visitor from the democracies in the encounter with state propaganda everywhere. The state communicates its control on radio, television, newspapers, film, art, billboards. Major industries are state-administered and even the peasants serve the state agricultural plans. The industrial workers, in whose name the revolution was conducted, fare better than their counterparts in India, but their condition does not compare to that of the workers of the middle-class democracies. It is not fair to compare the Russian workers' life-style to the American perhaps, but even in relative gains, since 1917 the American worker has outstripped the Russian counterpart in economic well-being, freedom, production, and personal security. More relevant is the comparison of the workers of Finland, who until 1917 were part of the Russian empire, to those of Russia immediately adjoining Finland. Another relevant comparison is East German workers to those of West Germany, from whom they were separated in 1945. In both Finland and West Germany, local workers have become middle class. The workers in Communist countries are better off than they were under the czars, but the workers' revolution has not accomplished as much as unionization, pragmatic adjustment, and political reform have in the democracies. The workers' paradise has not appeared and instead a state idolatry has emerged. Attempts by the democracies to attack directly this idolatry promise no more success and perhaps even greater cruelty than the Moslem and Christian attacks on India's polytheism. Neither Hinduism nor Marxism is going to collapse imminently; peacemaking will require dialogue to overcome their idolatrous tendencies.

The same sort of survey of the democratic mixed-economy societies reveals two idols that claim national resources and loyalty. The one

overwhelming idol is the amassing of personal wealth. This is most
.extreme in the United States with nearly a million millionaires, but
reducing life to financial success is not uncharacteristic of Swiss,
Germans, Dutch, and other nationalities. This drive for personal
wealth is blared out in the newspapers, literature, television, films,
and universities as the culture of the consuming society is propagated.
Salaries paid to the industrial managers soar beyond all reason as do
salaries paid to those who can advertise the products of the consuming
society through sport or entertainment. Americans are bombarded by
messages to consume and are taught avarice. Compared to much of
the rest of the world, America looks like middle-class paradise. The 20
percent failure rate of the society, represented by those who have not
achieved the income necessary to rise above the poverty line, is
neglected by those driven by the idol of personal wealth.

Governments are not very successful in organizing the production
of wealth in either India or in communist societies. Likewise in the
United States, but here the drive for wealth has bypassed the
government. There is little danger of government idolatry in the
United States. It is a continual struggle to get Americans to take the
government seriously. The personal drive for wealth produces a
pluralistic idolatry to the neglect of the state, although the second idol
involves the state. This is the idolatry of the national security function
of the state. The United States was unexpectedly left in a hegemonic
role in the world after the Second World War. As the rest of the world
recovered, America needed to surrender this artificial hegemony
gracefully and find her own role in the world as befitted a dynamic 6
percent of the world's population. Communism's threat to capitalism
and the fear of traditional Russian totalitarianism combined with
American pride to produce a pursuit of national security on the world
scene.

This idolatry of national security has led us into dangers of
unreasonable alliances with countries who share neither our values
nor our national interests. It has led us into a military stalemate on the
Korean peninsula, and into military defeat in Vietnam. Arming the
world, which of course reduces American power vis-à-vis the newly
armed, has become an American policy.

Out of fear, the leviathan of a national security organization has
evolved policies contrary to American democratic principles. Now the
leviathan threatens to destroy us all. The leviathan is armed beyond all
national needs. The arms themselves became the flashpoints of

danger, for example, in the Cuban missile crisis. Questions of the mobilization of forces led Europe into World War I. All of the great European empires should have been adequately deterred by others. But unsure of intentions and fearing the other gaining an advantage, Russia and Germany threw themselves into the fratricidal conflict, which destroyed their empires and initiated the decline of Europe.

The leviathan of the national security system reaches out for more than 6 percent of the G.N.P., draining the economy of its technological talents. In a fantasy of science fiction, it threatens now to arm space. As we finance wars from Lebanon and Afghanistan, to Nicaragua and Grenada, our chances for success seem less the reason for recourse to arms than the need for Leviathan to be involved in the conflicts. Can it be American pride that feeds Leviathan beyond rational American needs? If so, greed and pride stand as the human forces fueling Leviathan's threat to us all. From a biblical perspective, greed and pride are among the primary causes of war.

The trust in the idolatry of arms is specifically condemned in Scripture. If we ultimately trust in arms, we do not ultimately trust in God. Israel says in faith: "Some boast of chariots, and some of horses; but we boast of the name of the Lord our God" (Psalm 20:7). And the trust in armaments lead to war: "Because you have trusted in your chariots and in the multitude of your warriors, therefore the tumult of war shall arise among your people, and all your fortresses shall be destroyed" (Hosea 10:10b-14a).

Faith is trust in the ultimate graciousness of life. Faith is a human reality that is unequally shared. Erik Erikson has shown how it is given to infants as they receive security from their parents. As a human being develops, trust is encouraged or denied as life affects the growing being. Faith is not as much achieved as it is given. The baptism of children in most Christian churches affirms God's graciousness and entrusts the parents and the community to give this gift to the child.

The faith is an ultimate faith, it is a trust in the foundations of life. The other loyalties of life can be made relative. One does not need to put faith in local idols, in the state, in acquiring wealth, or in the national security system. They all are the work of our hands; they all will fail. Faith is the expression of Paul:

What then shall we say to this?
If God is for us, who is against us? (Romans 8:31)

In this faith (which led him to disrupt the state, the economy, and the idols at Ephesus), Paul found the peace that is the beginning of real peacemaking.

> Therefore, since we are justified by faith, we have *peace with God* through our Lord Jesus Christ. (Romans 5:1, emphasis mine)

Faith is the response of the person, and it is recognized as the foundation of peace in Islam as well as Judaism and Christianity. Islam knows that the whole social order is involved in peacemaking, but here too the role of faith in the person is central, as the Koran says: "Those who have faith and do not let it be debased by the least injustice are those who shall have peace. It is they who are on the right path" (6.83). Faith in Paul's religious crisis responded to the failure of Judaism, as he understood it, to achieve liberation through the law. In Luther, faith answered what the penitential system of Renaissance Roman Catholicism could not answer for him: the need for assurance of salvation. In our day faith overcomes the "meaninglessness of life," which has channeled life's energies into the idolatries of greed, statism, or militarism.

Faith is trust and not specifically belief. But in Christian life it is not trust in vagueness. It is trust in the one God known in power and goodness as the author of creation. Behind the evolving world of matter, energy, and life is a benevolent purpose seeking a free humanity's love. Goodness united with ultimate power is God, so although Christians fear power without goodness, the uniting of goodness and power is divine. The possibility of human life unfailingly responding in human power to God's graciousness is believed by Christians to have been realized in Jesus the Christ.

The Christ was expected in power, but he came as a servant and suffered. He was a teacher of morality, a healer, a founder of a community, and he realized the purpose of the universe in an unalienated life given completely to God. People responding to him have found peace and come to understand themselves as peacemakers. The Christian's trinitarian belief proclaims that the Spirit of God in Christ nurtures human life today. The Spirit, though never contradicting the picture of Jesus as the Christ, moves freely among human beings, nurturing faith and inspiring new forms of community among people. Many people testify to the knowledge that the spirit of Christian community transcending national and denominational barriers and in continuity with Christ is most real in peacemaking efforts.

Christian faith frees human beings to be human. The efforts of people to become minor deities are pathetic, and faith frees them from this impossible compulsion. On the other hand, some people are trying to become slaves to something or to someone else and faith frees them from this sacrifice of their humanity. In most areas of human endeavor, the fear of being a vulnerable human being drives people to pretend to be all-knowing, or perfectly moral, or all-powerful. In international politics nations act to fulfill the frail egos of their insecure people by maximizing power, judging other nations by their own particular standards and not those of the nation being judged, and by claiming absolute loyalties of the people. As the people surrender their human freedom to the politicians or the states, the nations become more dangerous and the people less human.

Humans are meant to be neither slaves nor gods. Yet in existing between slavery and divinity, they are tempted in their anxiety to surrender their humanity either to pretend to be the center of the universe or to another finite reality. The surrender of their humanity allows the pretenders to divinity to become more credible to themselves and to others, thereby increasing their pride.

Faith in God allows human beings to live as vulnerable human beings. They do not need to surrender their freedom to others, and they can resist tyranny and the claims of absolutism of various idols. It also breaks the pride of those who would claim absolute power, or knowledge, or morality. Faith in the absolute God makes other loyalties relative and reduces the temptation to destroy the world to protect an American understanding of free enterprise or a Russian understanding of communism. There is no need for holy wars, because the God who is holy desires peace. Faith is an antidote to greed and pride.

Feminist critiques of Christian theology have clarified an important point. Christian teaching by emphasizing self-sacrifice has mistakenly encouraged less than human life. People have been led to sacrifice their selves for the interests of others. There is a reality of self-sacrifice in Christian life, but it is the sacrifice of the old prideful self or the old idol-infested self to God, and one in faith receives a new self that can be free. By losing our old selves we are given new selves. Women particularly have been kept the poorest of the poor. There is nothing in Christian faith rightly understood that requires a sacrifice of them other than the sacrifice of that enslaved self so that they can be freed. In their becoming free the structures of all social relations are fundamentally shaken. As the woman abandons servitude she frees the man from the role of master. The oppressed and the oppressor both are freed; but of course, it is more difficult for the oppressor to see the more human quality of new, fairer structures of life.

Faith is exactly what the strife-torn world needs, for it encourages the oppressed to revolt for their true humanity. It allows the oppressors to help the revolt succeed for their true humanity. Faith allows justice to be arranged in ways that encourage the humanity of all to flourish. For in faith our meaning is not in wealth, consumption, position, or control, but in relationships to God and humanity. Faith does its work for peacemaking in the interiors of the human selves, allowing them to live freely without exploiting.

Of course, faith drives toward particular works for peacemaking. That is obvious. The world is in danger; the faithful will act. James put it clearly: "For as the body apart from the spirit is dead, so faith apart from works is dead" (James 2:26).

James did not remain abstract in his reference to works. His readers were warned against the injustice of riches. Faith that will not feed the hungry and clothe the naked is dead. His charge of "unfaithful creatures" is directed at those whose covetousness causes wars.

> What causes wars, and what causes fightings among you? Is it not your passions that are at war in your members? You desire and do not have; so you kill. And you covet and cannot obtain; so you fight and wage war. (James 4:1-2)

With millions hungry and a minority overfed, there is little chance for peace. The passions in ourselves lead to greed and to war; faith can counter those passions and create the humble person honored in James' letter. Yet his humble person is the one who carries out the works of kindness and righteousness: the healing, the feeding, and the clothing. These works require hope of fulfillment; faith undergirds hope and leads to hope.

Hope Not Armageddon

The references in preaching and in the remarks of President Reagan and former Secretary of Defense Weinberger to a final battle or a final nuclear holocaust called Armageddon reveal more about the speakers than about Scripture. The word *Armageddon* appears only once in the Bible. It is in the Greek of Revelation 16:16: "And they assembled them at the place which is called in Hebrew Armageddon." We cannot tell what this Hebrew word means since there is no other reference to such a word. It may refer to the mountain of Megiddo, but more likely, it refers to the Megiddo where Ahaziah died, perhaps to the city of Megiddo. It is possible that it refers to Jerusalem, since the context suggests Zion. But in any case the kings of the world were to be assembled there in this vision of judgment the author of John's revelation relates.

The next chapter removes any chronological confusion; the vision is explicitly about the destruction of the Roman Empire, which was persecuting Christians. Rome is judged, the rulers are listed, her burning is described, the collapse of commerce is detailed, and her allies are grief-stricken. Revelation, written in a time of Roman political persecution of Christians, has an explicit political theology that involves God overthrowing Rome and saving the people.

Actually of course, Rome was converted to Christianity before it was destroyed, but at the time of the writing of Revelation such a historical outcome would have seemed less probable than God's justice destroying Rome. Armageddon, this obscure word with its one biblical appearance, cannot bear the weight of nuclear theology. There is no biblical reason to think it has anything to do with nuclear war. To project a nuclear war on the basis of Revelation is to read into the text one's own fantasies. Revelation contains judgment, terrible judgment, but it concludes with a vision of a new earth and a new heaven, a restored city of peace. The Lamb is the prince of peace for whose coming Christians pray. The book is eschatologically optimistic for Christians who would read it and understand it in the midst of Roman persecution. The failure to read it and understand it in its historical setting, like the failure to understand the book of Daniel in the Old Testament, feeds fantasies and in the hands of people with power these can be dangerous. The historical settings are clear enough; once the apocalyptic language is understood the dangers are easily avoided.

The prophetic books are realistic about human suffering, and, as in Joel and Ezekiel, those who have done violence to Jerusalem suffer for it. In most of the books, the final pattern is that of Isaiah or Amos; Israel will be restored in righteousness and peace. "The mountains shall drip sweet wine, and all the hills shall flow with it. I will restore the fortunes of my people Israel, and they shall rebuild the ruined cities and inhabit them" (Amos 9:13d-14b).

Jeremiah prophesied the destruction of Jerusalem. He saw the ravishing of the small countries of the fertile crescent. He even announced the coming destruction of Babylon. Yet even in Jeremiah the oracles of peace are heard. He criticizes those who promise peace before it is to come. He has little use for cheap comfort. However, he realistically advises the Hebrews going into exile: "Seek the *shalom* of the city where I have sent you into exile, and pray to the Lord on its behalf, for in its *shalom* you will find your *shalom*" (Jeremiah 29:7; the RSV translates *shalom* as welfare). He spurns the illusions of those who promise Judah a quick return, but then he gives a word of hope: "For I know the plans I have for you, says the Lord, plans for *shalom* and not for evil, to give you a future and a hope" (Jeremiah 29:11). The historical details, of course, are not our own details. No literal or even analogous reading is intended. But there is a theology of realistic hope here that is affirmed. Life is tough, but we are to seek peace in the city where we are destined to exist. The Lord's plan, the intention of the universe, is to give a future, not evil, but a hope.

Christians daily pray "Thy Kingdom come," which means may the order of justice and peace be established in historical fact or "on earth as it is in God's reign" or "in heaven." The Kingdom has started and each Christian can tell of moments of the realization of the reign of God, yet Christians long for its fulfillment.

Romans 8:22 captures the basic Christian eschatology of realistic hope as well as any single New Testament text:

> We know that the whole creation has been groaning in travail together until now; and not only the creation, but we ourselves, who have the first fruits of the Spirit, groan inwardly as we wait for adoption as [children], the redemption of our bodies. For in this hope we were saved. (Romans 8:22-24a)

The hope is not a hope that turns one way from the world's travail. Persecution is expected, but the Christian living in hope will seek peace, and refrain from returning evil with evil. Evil will be overcome with good.

Christian eschatology like Hebrew eschatology is rooted in the historical conditions of the time of its writing; it is meant to reinforce Christian practice, and it is hopeful, not despairing. Eschatological

formulations of our time are faithful to Scripture by expressing the
hope of Scripture, by being rooted in the agony of our time, and by
encouraging historical action. The Committee of the World Council
of Churches, which held hearings on nuclear weapons in 1983,
understood the relevance of eschatology. The committee counseled
Christians facing the apocalyptic dimensions of nuclear warfare
against responses of fatalism, facile optimism, or the abandonment of
faith. Holding to the World Council of Churches' stance of hopeful
activism, the committee affirmed:

> We believe that the authentic Christian response to such threats is to
> accept our calling to be fellow-workers with Christ in the redemption of
> the world from evil. Our mandate is to go on praying, believing,
> working and hoping, no matter how daunting the task.[1]

Hope Inspires Action

Ethics assumes hope because ethics is about what we ought to do. It is
reflection on future-oriented action. It assumes action toward the future
makes a difference. The future is open to a degree. The inquiry into
peacemaking focuses practically on American-Russian relations, the
requirement of saying no to nuclear weapons, the human rights
struggle, the issues of revolution and counterrevolution, and development. In all of these areas, the past has shaped our alternatives, but the
alternatives are there, and we as humans may choose and act. Our
actions cannot eliminate the ambiguities of our historical heritage, but
they can eliminate particular forms of evil. In our free actions within
history we become more human. As we become more human we
become more hopeful even if the struggle prevents us from relinquishing
realistic appreciation of the opposition.

The American civil rights movement expressed hope in the dream
of Martin Luther King, Jr., of a beloved community. For a time he
achieved a transforming beloved community in the Southern
Christian Leadership Conference. He united the realism of the pain
of the black experience with the power of hopeful black preaching. I
marched with him in the 1960s, but only later would I come to know
how profound a church social strategist he was. In 1963 I did not know
how necessary eschatological hope was to mobilizing the forces that
beat upon Washington wave after wave until finally the sand castles of
bigotry surrendered and legal discrimination was ended. It is because

evil is so entrenched that hope must be so full. The cadences of the "I Have a Dream" speech still roll through my ears from that hot Washington day before the Lincoln Memorial. The specifics of the dream have not been fulfilled, but a particular evil was defeated. Particular legislation was passed.

The clash with the administration over Vietnam and the deepening struggle with the FBI created the climate and the opportunity for his murder. His strategies of using the American dream, the power of black worship services, and tactics of nonviolence acceptable to the churches were abandoned. But the dreams were resurrected in the United Nations stances of today's Atlanta Mayor, Andrew Young, Democratic presidential aspirant Jesse Jackson, and in the deepening of the worldwide concern for human rights stemming from the Jimmy Carter presidency. Evil is not eliminated but victories have been won, more are winnable, and the struggle is beautiful.

For those of us who are perpetual volunteers in the peace movement, hope is seen in our children surviving and coming into the movement also. Particular wars that could have been fought have been avoided, wars that could have spread have been contained, and we have lived forty years without any more atomic destruction of cities. Secular planners and nuclear eschatologists are now agreeing that nuclear war cannot be fought. We may be approaching a point of emerging consensus that the nuclear danger must now be contained. Christian churches are being joined by Hindus, Moslems, Buddhists, and others in deepening their concern for peace. There are signs of hope.

The motivations inspired by the threats of complete nuclear destruction are fearful. Sometimes Christians in the peace movement decry the motivation of fear, arguing instead for inspiration grounded solely in hope. The fear is inevitable, it is a human reality that cannot be ignored. This mixed motivation is profoundly correlated with biblical eschatology, which is usually a mixture of both fear and hope. The message today is, fear the evil consequences of our structured-fearful militarism and hope for actions of peacemaking that will turn the forces of history away from nuclear apocalypse and toward structures of social justice. Edward Schillebeeckx links our hopes with our actions:

> Christian theologians must revitalize this concept of the Kingdom of God, not seen as a kind of other-world Kingdom of God, but as a

beginning to be realized in this world, here and now. There must be a positive link between our human acting in social, political, and economic affairs and the coming of the Kingdom of God.[2]

One of the significant actions of hope is that nations with the capacity to build nuclear weapons have refrained. Some have built them secretly, expanding the nuclear cabal to include South Africa and Israel. Brazil, Argentina, India, and Pakistan have so far not developed weapons. The link between reactors for research and for electrical energy and nuclear weapons is so close that containing the spread of the weapons is largely a matter of national renunciation. India's self-restraint is tested by the presence of American nuclear weapons in the Indian Ocean, Chinese and Russian nuclear weapons to the immediate north, and the threat of the development of nuclear weapons in her arch-enemy Pakistan. The success of the Israeli strike against the French-built reactor in Iraq incited Pakistanis to fear that India would strike Pakistan's facilities before weapons were built. So far, restraint has governed her actions. We in the Western world that has been unable to muster corresponding self-restraint are impressed by this Indian achievement. India has many problems, but so far she does not contribute to the threat of the madness of nuclear holocaust. From India comes the voice of a Christian ethicist, Somen Das, who finds hope and signs of the reign of God in actions in the world. In the protests against nuclear weapons in Hyde Park, London, and in West Germany, he saw signs of a new future. Quoting Aleksandr Solzhenitsyn, "A shout in the mountains has been known to create an avalanche," he urged action to avert the drift toward the nuclear holocaust:

> So we can anticipate the future not on the basis of the present reality. In the final analysis *it is not so much a matter of anticipation but of participation.* Then nuclear war is not a matter of inevitability but the possibility of change becomes real and concrete.[3]

Our hopeful biblical eschatology leads to participation in the struggle for peace. There have been those who have suggested God's will might include the nuclear destruction of the world. But this is impossible. The foremost commandment for human life is "To love thy neighbor as thyself." There can be no nuclear destruction that does not violate this commandment. To acquiesce to nuclear fatalism is to surrender Christian ethics and to deny Jesus as a teacher of ethics. Given our hopeful eschatology: What are we in love to do?

Active Love Seeking Peacemaking

In Paul's summary of the Christian life as faith, hope, and love, love is the love of neighbor. This is clear, since in Galatians he writes: "For the whole law is fulfilled in one word, 'You shall love your neighbor as yourself' " (Galatians 5:14). Paul is quoting Leviticus: "You shall not take vengeance or bear any grudge against the sons of your own people, but you shall love your neighbor as yourself: I am the Lord" (Leviticus 19:18). Paul, of course, is not rejecting the tradition Jesus taught, shared in Mark 12, Luke 10, and Matthew 22, that the summary of the law was in two commandments.

> You shall love the Lord your God with all your heart, and with all your soul, and with all your mind. This is the great and first commandment. And a second is like it, You shall love your neighbor as yourself. On these two commandments depend all the law and the prophets. (Matthew 22:37-40)

In Mark and Luke the commonality of this tradition to Judaism is recognized as in these witnesses the proper understanding is attributed first to a scribe and then to a lawyer. Paul, writing earlier than Matthew, Mark, or Luke, probably did not know of this strong tradition associating Jesus with a twofold commandment. Actually the "Love of God" in the first commandment is the virtue of faith in Paul's threefold summary and his *love* corresponds to the love of neighbor of the second commandment.

The meaning of this love is the active pursuit of the neighbor's real well-being. It is to care and act for the other as we would care and act for ourselves. This love requirement, rooted in the faith of God's love for humanity and in hope of God's purposes for humanity, is the foundation of Christian action. The meaning of love for Jesus is shown in his true teaching, in his real healing, and in his actual feeding. The Samaritan demonstrates love by acting for the well-being of the hurt traveler. The believer acts in love for Paul by clothing and feeding. Paul's letters are full of the meaning of love as he pleads for collections of money to provide for the suffering saints of Jerusalem. "Let all that you do be done in love" (I Corinthians 16:14).

Shalom or biblical peace means that both peace and mutual

concord and justice are fair relationships. There is a dialectical mutuality between this peace and justice. You cannot have one without the other. Love requires both. We can love in a world without much peace or much justice. In fact it is such a world in which we learn of love and accept its obligations. But love requires peace and justice in that in its active pursuing character it reaches in hope for both peace and justice.

Justice serves love as fair relationships structure the possibility of the neighbor's well-being. Paul Tillich's understanding of justice as the social forms in which beings can fulfill themselves is correct but a little idealistic. Reinhold Niebuhr's understanding of justice as a tolerable balance of power in which beings do not destroy one another's vitalities is more realistic. Of course, in reality we have not achieved a tolerable degree of justice. The Christian life, in being motivated by God's love, is a struggle for a tolerable approximation of justice. Realistically the point needs to be recognized that Christianity is not radically egalitarian. Christian faith is more concerned about all contributing to well-being and everyone receiving what is actually needed than it is about absolute equality. Even when the early Christians held their property in common, they distributed it according to need (Acts 2:45; 4:35) and eliminated poverty in their community. But this reservation about absolute egalitarianism does not imply that the present arrangements even begin to approximate justice. Life opportunities in the democratic nations of the NATO alliance are not distributed justly. Particularly in the United States the gap between those born rich and those born poor is a shocking denial of justice. There is no equal opportunity for the extremes. There may be an approximate justice among the middle class, but here the opportunities of males and females and of whites and blacks violate any standard of justice. But the opportunities of the middle class are dwarfed by the opportunities of the fabulously rich, who dominate decision making in the country.

Even Communism seems unable to achieve rough social justice, since special privileges inevitably drift toward those with political power. This recognition of gross inequality in Communist society is not recorded in a spirit of gloating, but in a spirit of sadness. The world would be a better place if Communism had been able to achieve greater equality than it has. Its sacrifice of freedom is hardly justified as new classes of privilege emerge.

But of course, the greatest violations of justice as fairness occur in the poor two thirds of the world. The poor southern nations, which contain the majority of the world's population, are characterized by extreme riches and extreme poverty. Certainly the poverty of the south is owing to being exploited by their colonial masters and their current economic masters. Decisions made in New York, Amsterdam, Paris, and Moscow are hardly made for the poor in the southern nations. Nor do the elites of the southern nations serve their poor. The policies of Buenos Aires, Mexico City, Delhi, and Tehran cannot be said to be made in the interests of the poor.

A Just Peace

Love inspires the struggle for justice and peace. Both are social expressions of the meaning of love. Yet justice and peace are far removed from historical reality.

Niebuhr followed John XXIII in naming justice as the goal while love was the motive of Christian action. In regard to the intentional arena, love seeks a just peace. The goal is ahead, but we live our lives and fashion our strategies toward that goal. The kingdom of God is not yet realized, but because of a taste of it we act for it and against the forces opposed to it. The present strategic needs may be to prevent the present world contradictions from destroying humanity until these contradictions are overcome. So out of love Christians act toward a just peace, the realization of which they do not expect in their history; yet they act for the survival and further development of human history.

A just peace would be one in which the two ideological systems of the superpowers, if they were still extant, could compete without threatening each other's children with nuclear destruction. A just peace presupposes the adoption of the United States of a no-first-use policy and reciprocal adjustments by the Soviet Union in strategic planning, the realization of a comprehensive test ban treaty, and the beginning of significant cuts in nuclear arsenals. The reduction of cold war pressures will help other nations to experiment with a rich variety of religions, philosophies, values, economics, and social systems.

The educational and health expenditures of the nations of the world would have supplanted expenditures of national security as national priorities. International institutions of order would be developing and the once dominant powers would be diminishing their competitive influence in maintaining order. The United States' reluctance to submit cases to the World Court would have been overcome and international institutions would be strengthening the sinews of world community.

Human rights consensus would be emerging and totalitarian barriers to political and religious rights would have crumpled. Economic rights would no longer be feared as an instrument of the cold war rivalry, the United States would have signed the human rights covenants, and the mixed economies would have demonstrated compassion in practice. Freed from militarism, the countries of the developing world would tend to use *satyagraha* in the Gandhian tradition and nonviolent resistance in the Christian civil rights tradition to resist tyranny and to move governments toward democracy and development.

Diplomacy and negotiations would be used more in international conflicts. Armed force would be relied on less as the world moved toward a just peace. Gradually the need for military forces along borders would atrophy and disarmament could follow. More and more unguarded borders like the Canadian-United States border would appear. More and more countries would no longer draw up new war plans against former perceived enemies as the old plans became redundant.

A just peace movement would not necessarily have achieved a world government, but the need for institutions of world order supplanting nuclear terror would have been recognized. The dialogue among world belief systems to find the understandings of world community would have received a priority in energy and funding. Some movement toward an appropriate equivalent of Isaiah's "lawgiver from Zion" would be recognized.

The United Methodist bishops in their pastoral paper of 1986 listed twenty principles or guidelines for a just peace.[4] The listing is reminiscent of the listing of principles for a just war. The foregoing attempt is to present a picture of a possible future. It is not meant to represent a utopia or the kingdom of God, but a possible future if humanity is wise and fortunate. It is intended not as law, but as the lure of a future. It is not a future that we will simply be given; in part it is ours to make. Other pictures of a just peace are described by Edward L. Long, Jr., and his own work is a projection of helpful actions for a just peace.[5] Out of several efforts to think about just peace can emerge a consensus. This picture attempts to remain realistic and to account for resistance to peacemaking while motivating action. We are now at the beginning of peace thinking, but we have a long way to go before we are clear on the agreed-upon ecumenical understanding of a just peace. Michael Walzer's outstanding book *Exodus and Revolution* eschews utopianism and concludes on a note that describes the development of an ethic of realism for peacemaking.

The lesson of the remarkable actions of liberation recorded in Exodus testify to faith and organization to defeat even the gods and power of Egypt meaning bondage and oppression. The lessons are:

—first, that wherever you live, it is probably Egypt;
—second, that there is a better place, a world more attractive, a promised land;
—and third, that "the way to the land is through the wilderness." There is no way to get from here to there except by joining together and marching.[6]

IV. REALISM, HUMAN RIGHTS, AND FOREIGN POLICY

In Christian teaching and in practical politics, human rights are intrinsically connected to peacemaking. This is so in Christian teaching because the very meaning of peace in its biblical expressions contains the relationships that permit full human development. Both the World Council of Churches and the Vatican's teachings on peace always include human rights as part of peacemaking. It is so in practical politics as the drive to realize human rights propels oppressed people into revolutionary actions. Within the United States, debates about human rights intersect the formation of policies for the cold war, for South Africa, and for Central America.

Full human rights are everywhere denied. The story of human rights is one of the struggle of true humanity to be realized. Human rights are the recognition that the meaning of human has its guarantees in a realm beyond the human empirical reality. Humans strive for, sometimes demand, and sometimes fight for the conditions under which a fuller approximation of the human can be found.

Human rights are found in three categories. In the philosophical category the meaning of human contains certain demands or rights for human life. In the historical category human rights are the subject matter of controversy and struggle. In the eschatological category, rights are expressions or goals of human existence; their realization is promised in the fulfillment of history, at the end of history, or beyond history.

The human rights issue exploded in the debates about the foreign

Part of this chapter was delivered as a paper at the Society of Christian Ethics' annual meeting, Washington, D.C., January 16, 1982. Michael Novak, the U.S. representative to the Human Rights Commission, responded and a dialogue followed.

policy of Jimmy Carter. Drawing on his Baptist tradition, Reinhold Niebuhr, and the Civil Rights movement, he pushed the moral demands of human rights into United States foreign policy. The application of the policy had consequences around the world but particularly as it intersected revolutionary struggles in Iran, Southern Africa, and Central America. A United Church of Christ minister in the tradition of Martin Luther King, Jr., Ambassador Andrew Young carried the banner until the controversy became too rancorous and he was forced out.

Neoconservatives attacked President Carter's human rights policy, attempted to discredit it, and chose to support candidate Ronald Reagan. In the early Reagan administration the neoconservatives were pushed forward to administer the human rights aspects of U.S. foreign policy. The Senate balked at the opponent of Carter's human rights record and denied the nomination of Ernest Lefever as Assistant Secretary of State for Human Rights. In this debate the intersection of religious ideas and politics in the human rights struggle is clearly seen. Before examining this debate (which poses the issues of realism, human rights, and peacemaking), attention to the origin of the concept of human rights is required.

Different nations represent different traditions in human rights. Though they covenant together in the Universal Declaration of Human Rights (1948)[1] or in the Helsinki Final Act (1975), they read their joint declarations from their own perspectives. This chapter focuses on a Western-American reading of the origins of human rights. This is a radically different story of the origins of human rights from the stories of other nations. A recent essay on the Hindu tradition of human rights, for example, described the interpretation and development of the understanding of the great collection of Hindu law of Manu's *Dharma Sutra*. Rammohan Roy, Vivekananda, Rabindranath Tagore, and most of all Gandhi broadened the understanding of human rights.[2] These contributions are vital to understanding current Indian perspectives on human rights, but they were only indirectly relevant to the West's development of its tradition. The indirect influence is almost entirely owing to Gandhi and his appropriation by the civil rights movement in the United States. Gandhi's own use of Western religious concepts in his Hindu system points to the emerging synthesis, which is not yet realized in human rights thinking. As Gandhi could not have been Gandhi without Jesus, so the Carter human rights policies could not have been without

Martin Luther King, Jr. Hence they too depended on Gandhi. India's participation in the human rights debate has owed something to the socialist tradition and to British political thought, especially utilitarianism. Similarly, each country's participation is very complex because its traditions both are uniquely its own and in some aspects belong to the world.

Within the United States at least three traditions compete and interrelate as they contribute to human rights consciousness. The Roman Catholic tradition[3] draws upon Thomas Aquinas and papal teaching to ground human rights in natural law. Such a tradition is neglected by philosophers of human rights like Ronald Dworkin[4] and A. I. Melden,[5] who engage Jeremy Bentham and John Locke respectively as conversational partners. The third tradition, the one of primary interest for this case, is the Protestant tradition. In this case it was the tradition grounded primarily in a Protestant reading of scripture and the political history of the Western world that was at issue.

Universal Standards in Ninth Century B.C.

The demand for equal treatment arises early in human consciousness. It can be seen in our children. But the natural inequalities among people and contingencies give rise to inequalities, which the powerful enforce and gradually the weaker accept and internalize. To treat others as one desires to be treated is the foundation of morality. It is recognized that each one counts as one and only one. To root this natural sense of morality in universal standards and to require it as the will of a just God is more complicated.

Ancient Hebrew experience, politics, and revelation led them through covenantal experience, resistance to landed oligarchs, and the experience of relative freedom in their hills to develop a sense of justice. In an explosion of radical monotheism, Amos would express this sense of justice or righteousness in terms that judged the inhuman conduct of all nations. This radically free, agricultural laborer living in a village on the desert side of Jerusalem understood that all nations were under God's universal judgment. From Amos comes a trajectory of universal standards anchored in God's will. The force of this proclamation would be bent, suppressed, and ignored in the rest of Israel's history and in the life of the church, but it would reappear whenever the sense of radical monotheism, the corruption of the present, the possibility of a more just future, and the reality of God having a will for human life intersected.

Amos did not speak of human rights, but his criticism of inhuman conduct outlines what he regarded as God's protection of human life. Damascus was condemned for destroying Gilead, Gaza was condemned for exiling a people and delivering them to another land, Tyre was condemned for surrendering a people to Edom and for not remembering *"the covenant of brotherhood"* (Amos 1:9, emphasis mine). Edom was punished for not showing pity and for ruthlessness, the Ammonites were punished for attacking women with child, and Moab for desecrating the remains of royal dead. Judah was to be punished for not keeping the law of the Lord. Where the covenant of the Lord was known it was wrong not to keep it. In the other countries a more general *"covenant of brotherhood"* was referred to or specific violations were named. Then even his host nation of Israel was condemned to punishment for selling people for profit, for oppressing the poor, for not comforting the suffering, for sexual misuse of women, and for misusing wine in the sanctuary.

Amos clearly sees God rejecting war atrocities, the selling of people, sexual exploitation, the oppression of the poor, and violations of human compassion. This very rigorous standard seen in the oracles of chapters 1 and 2 of Amos could not go unchallenged. The criticism was too much, and especially when Amos in Bethel specifically prophesied the downfall of the Kingdom because of its corruption, he was opposed by the authorities, particularly the high priest Amaziah. A high religious authority can always be found to protect political authorities from the criticism of prophetic religious teaching. Amaziah ordered Amos to stop his preaching since Bethel was the king's chapel and the king's royal residence. Amos could only reply that he was not a professional prophet but merely an agricultural laborer and that God's justice meant that Israel's atrocities doomed her. She would be destroyed in war.

Certainly the sense that one of the prerequisites of peace is the ending of the violation of human dignity is as old as Amos' ninth-century B.C. prophecy. The promises for Israel's restoration are: to achieve economic security, the capacity to build cities and to inhabit them, to plant crops and to enjoy the fruit, and to inhabit their homeland safely.

Amos is referred to here in order to note the theological grounding of universal standards, the political-religious suppression of critics of the violations of humanity, the threat to the state of humanitarian criticism, and the political arena of the struggle for human dignity. In Amos we can see that the source of our life forbids the rulers of the world to practice injustice, that the achievement of justice eludes us, and that the attempt to promote justice across international borders is full of peril. The roots of human rights go back to the religious transcendence of kingly rule in Israel and to the development of a critical ethic on the grounds of radical monotheism.

In Amos, a standard of justice rooted in the will of the *one* God for the one humanity was used to criticize other nations. That very standard led Amos into trouble when he took it into the royal palace of his neighboring state Israel. The conflict is very suggestive of the debate over human rights policy for contemporary foreign policy.

Other Sources

Before we move into an analysis of the current human rights debate, the complexity of the sources of human rights claims needs to be recognized. Max L. Stackhouse has traced this history of human rights in his major study *Creeds, Society, and Human Rights: A Study in Three Cultures.*[6]

The roots of human rights in the Hebrew conception of a just God were nourished by the prophets and the social-religious bonding of the "covenants." Through the life of the Jewish people and the organization of the synagogue, the tradition was expressed in the humanizing teaching of Jesus and in recognition of a universal law of conscience by Paul. As the early church evolved from the synagogue it incorporated Greek trajectories of concern for the protection of the human. Stoic doctrines of equality merged with Christian conceptions of faith, hope, and love to form a vision of human life that survived the persecution of the church. If one follows Professor Stackhouse's recognition of the Council of Constance in A.D. 1415 as the birth of modernity, then we have a period of 1,005 years from the sacking of Rome in 410 during which the church sought religious freedom for itself and the protection of the rights of the Christian person from oppression. Yet the church's defensiveness against the real enemies of both Islam and Christian emperors drove it into its own forms of repression. The West merged from the medieval period with two realms of authority—church and state—and an emerging realm of economic energy. In the space provided by the freedom of the church would emerge the voluntary associations of the liberal-reformed world, which have contributed to modern forms of human rights. The thought of the High Middle Ages also contributed Thomas Aquinas' natural law theory, which could serve as the basis for Catholic thinking on human rights in the modern period. In the East, John Chrysostom and Basil defended the rights of the poor and opposed the luxury of the rulers. Basil's argument for the recognition of essential human equality was grounded, as all Christian arguments for human dignity are, on the image of God in humanity.[7] In this Orthodox history were laid the grounds for contemporary Orthodox commitments to human rights.

The Renaissance and the Reformation contributed to the liberation of the European mind in different ways and to individualism in European life. Humanity sprung into autonomous forms of life that took expression in the struggle for diverse forms of religious-intellectual expression. The Calvinist, Lutherans, and Anabaptists all expressed slightly different versions of humanity, which Europe finally had to tolerate. Covenantal political theory and the emergence of social contract theory both deepened the commitment to human rights including individual rights by social bonding.

The Modern Situation

In modern history the expression of human rights has been to limit the state. This was first asserted to protect the rights of Englishmen (Petition of Rights, 1628, and Bill of Rights, 1689). These ideas are reflected in the later more universal sounding French Declaration of the Rights of Man and the American Bill of Rights.

The ground for the post–World War II Universal Declaration of Human Rights in 1948 was prepared by writing on international concern for human rights (Francisco de Vitoria, 1480–1546), the emergence of international law as perceived as resting on grounds of a universal law of humanity, the practice of "humanitarian intervention," and the development of protection for groups by treaty.[8]

This work on developing a body of proclamations on human rights continues in the work of the United Nations and its specialized agencies as well as through regional organizations. The work suffers because it lacks either the clear theological rationale that declarations of the World Council of Churches or pronouncements of the Vatican reflect or the power suggested by governmental declarations. Agreement on clear philosophical principles seems to be as elusive as the attempt to achieve theological unity would be divisive.

The pronouncements of these international bodies, then, have little authority. They represent majority vote positions on issues of human concern. Individual countries adopt their respective positions for diverse philosophical and political reasons. They have the authority of diverse council or commission statements on social ethical issues without the councils being responsible for policy or implementation.

Within U.S. foreign policy concerns, the ambiguities that Alexander Hamilton noted about the Bill of Rights appear. He thought that it was more naturally appropriate to have a bill of rights in a treatise on ethics than in a constitution of a government. The human rights issue is a place where the power concerns of people and the ethical expressions of people find a meeting place. This chapter traces part of that ambiguous meeting in recent United States concerns about human rights and foreign policy. If we had a world government, Hamilton notwithstanding, a bill of rights would be very necessary. To have a declaration of rights before the government is established is to leave it with the force of a moral statement arrived at by compromise.

The United States' contribution to the human rights struggle has been hindered by two factors central to the meaning of the country. Slavery was only overcome after being recognized by the constitution and building wealth in the country. The fruits of slavery continued even after the Civil War in the failure of the United States to treat its black minority justly. The very human rights policy of the government is fruit of the struggle against the racial blight of the nation. Prejudices and discrimination continue and prevent the human rights policies from advancing.

In addition to slavery, the United States had in its beginnings a significant expression of human autonomy. The old heteronomous structures of Europe were overthrown. The myths of the radically self-determining person flourished. The social bonding of the Puritans was gradually abandoned, and the Yankee emerged. Once this autonomous individual came to believe in the myths of Social Darwinism, a socially irresponsible, technically powerful individual was let loose on the world. Whether this type evolves into the conquering, hedonistic-utilitarian or the escapist, hedonistic-expressionist, the realities of a social bond that structures human rights were dissolved. So typically the American believes he or she has freedom in a mass-produced consumer autonomy and resents all social bonding as eclipsing freedom.[9]

The strengthening of the biblical and democratic concepts of social responsibility in American culture are a necessary part of the struggle for human rights. Without the social ideas and social reality, human rights sound like moralism. Then the temptation to use it as a moralistic weapon in the cold war arises. Used as a cold war weapon, human rights are neither felt in the way one lives in the world nor are they meaningfully articulated.

The development of the human rights strategy in the early Reagan administration revealed this confusion. Human rights were seen on the one hand as extraneous ideals foreign to politics and on the other as symbols to be used in the cold war.

The Nomination of an Assistant Secretary of State for Human Rights

The minutes of the Senate Foreign Relations Committee hearings on the nomination of Ernest Lefever provide an excellent case study in the difficulties of applying religious social ethics to foreign policy issues. The senators, the nominee, and the witnesses reveal both their ethics of being and their ethics of doing. The character of the nominee is probed, examined, criticized, and praised. His decisions and writings are analyzed both for their ethical sensitivity and their political content. The ambiguity of life and its expression in ethics and foreign policy is dramatically portrayed.

Lefever's claim to stand in the tradition of Reinhold Niebuhr introduced the meaning of Niebuhr's perspective in the Senate debate. Sometimes the relevance of Niebuhr's thought and what he meant or had not meant seemed to be as much the subject of inquiry as the interpretation of Ernest Lefever's thought. However, both those who favored and those who opposed Lefever's nomination claimed Niebuhr as one of their mentors in thinking about ethics and foreign policy. The testimony of Michael Novak, the chief of the delegation to the United Nations Human Rights Commission, also emphasized the influence of Niebuhr on both his own thought and that of the nominee he supported. Lefever's record of criticism of the human rights perspective of Jimmy Carter, Andrew Young, and Martin

Luther King, Jr., all of whom had acknowledged their debt to Reinhold Niebuhr, only reveals the complexity of the questions concerning the position of Christian realism on foreign policy and human rights. A major variable in the positions taken during the hearing was the various attitudes toward the cold war. Judgments about how human rights issues should be effected in the situation of the cold war were as important as any other variable in the discussion except for judgments about the character of the witness and his own conduct in the Ethics and Public Policy Center regarding Nestle Corporation and the funding of the center.

Niebuhr on Human Rights

Reinhold Niebuhr's writing on human rights often appears under the themes of social justice and international relations or on particular comments on problems in foreign policy.[10] In summary he taught that the origins of human rights rested on humanity's freedom because humanity was created in the image of God. The human struggle has been, in part, to realize in its political life the capacities of freedom rooted in the essential quality of humanity. These expressions of human freedom, which are difficult to contain in political communities, which enrich the community in the long run.[11] So a tension exists in all societies between the forces that order society and the expression of human freedom, which transcends all particular political order. In this perspective the struggle for the freedoms enshrined in Western history in the Magna Charta, the Bill of Rights, the Declaration of the Rights of Man, and the Declaration of Human Rights represents a continuing quest for the conditions that will allow for the freedom of human nature. Particular expressions of norms for protecting human rights are contingent, even political, declarations that reflect more or less accurately the need for human nature to be protected in its quest for expression of its freedom. The perspective could be thought of as a relative natural law expression. The law of human nature is to express its freedom; the human perceptions of that freedom are contingent on the perceptions of those fighting for human freedom. So Thomas Jefferson could assert that the God who gave us life gave us freedom, while not becoming cognizant of the implication of that for all members of the human species. Or Alexander Hamilton could, with most males until recently, declare we have sacred rights written in human nature by divinity itself while being blind to the need for the female expression of freedom.

For Niebuhr, the realization of tolerable conditions of justice meant a social arrangement that would allow members of the society to express their vitalities without infringing on the rights of others. Therefore, justice depended on the social institutions of a particular society more than it did on abstract pronouncements.

His social philosophy combined passion for social justice, seen in his lifelong campaign for rights for minorities and for the rights of workers in his society, and a recognition of the forces that resisted social justice. This dual recognition is what caused him to resist idealistic posturing while still struggling for justice. He regarded this combination as part of the mixture of the English revolution and found in it one of the best expressions of Christian social action.

> There was, for instance, Ireton's shrewd observation that he preferred "the rights of Englishmen to the rights of man," meaning that a mutually acknowledged right and responsibility was a more reliable guarantee of justice than abstractly conceived "inalienable rights." All the superiority of a common law tradition, of an unwritten constitution, and a history in which "liberty broadens down from precedent to precedent" is expressed in this preference.[12]

The sense of the contingency of human rights in the Western world encouraged doubt about the protection of human rights in societies that lacked a religious sense of the worth of human selfhood. Individualism in the West had been extravagant in many expressions, but still the appreciation of the worth of the individual pointed toward certain factors as necessary for the protection of human rights. Institutional guarantees of a free judicial system with a veto over policies and rulers, and guarantees of freedom of expression, were perceived as minimally necessary to protect human rights.[13] These institutional guarantees had to be buttressed by a sense of the broader community, intellectual competence of the electorate, and a balance of power in the economic realm. Niebuhr was aware of the struggle within different communist states and authoritarian states to realize some of these factors, but he was not at all sanguine about their realization.

Human rights were continually challenged in countries heir to Western democratic traditions and on the world scene as a whole. Human rights remains more of an ideal than a reality. American society still denies American blacks rights and hinders the development of their capacities. There are only approximations of human rights, but still they are to be contended for and institutionalized in law, practice, and economic opportunity.

The promise of justice was a major factor in the competition between the Soviet Union and the United States. Niebuhr saw the competition going on for decades and a first priority was managing the competition in a way to prevent nuclear war. He welcomed the competition ideologically and, while regarding the extravagant promises of laissez faire capitalism and Marxism as both badly flawed myths, he thought the Marxist myth would have more rapid acceptance in the recently decolonized world. His critique of the Marxist myth and of Soviet practice was part of this ideological warfare, and he hoped that in the long run the achievements of the Western nations in realizing an approximation of justice would assist the new nations in refusing to succumb to the blandishments of the Soviet empire.

Niebuhr was a little extravagant in his expectations for Kennedy's Alliance for Progress, but he certainly thought it was important for the United States to set aside some of the liberal reservations about intervention for the sake of encouraging land reform and education in Latin America. He also personally participated in the withdrawal of accounts from the United States banks that supported the consortium efforts to increase South Africa's credit after the Sharpeville massacre. He confided to me on one of our walks how it was slightly embarrassing to meet one of the vice presidents of Chemical Bank on Riverside Drive, after he in supporting the bank campaign organized by Union Seminary students had withdrawn his account, as had *Christianity and Crisis*. Niebuhr also implied that he believed the bank official agreed with the action personally and morally, though institutionally he supported his bank's policy. The achievement of justice was both a good to be struggled for in its own terms and an issue in cold war competition. Authority in the modern world rested on this expectation of justice, and innovative ways to promote it were to be encouraged.

Of course, he resisted abstract democratic idealism as well, particularly when it was mixed with self-inflating calculations of political interest. His major critiques of self-righteousness in 1967 and 1968 were directed at the shallow rhetoric of defending democracy and self-determination in Vietnam.[14]

In summary: He regarded social justice as a major issue in the competition of the two empires in the cold war. It was a goal he had struggled for throughout his own life, it was grounded in humanity as a creation of God, it could be misused, and a nation had to be aware of the dangers of moral and spiritual pride. Social justice would not be perfectly realized in history, and prudence and passion were both necessary in the effort to approximate its realization.

The Carter Human Rights Attempt

Michael Novak and Ernest Lefever both criticized the Carter administration's approach to human rights. In both cases, the major criticism was that the Carter policy neglected to attack the violation of human rights in the "totalitarian" societies sufficiently and that it was too hard on U.S. allies who were practicing "authoritarian" government.

Novak summarized the development of the human rights policy, noting how both Senator Jackson and Senator Moynihan had argued that human rights was an instrument that should be used critically against the Soviet Union. Carter was portrayed as neglecting the advantage the human rights issue gave the United States over the Soviet Union and in falsifying "the meaning of human rights."

> The Carter Administration turned this human rights policy inside out. It did not make human rights a policy of truth. It did not make human rights a policy of political advantage. . . . Thus, the Carter Administration made an attempt to be "evenhanded," and to balance every accusation against an opponent of the United States with an accusation against a friend.[15]

Lefever stressed the importance of the distinction between "authoritarian" and "totalitarian" regimes again and again in his testimony before the Senate Foreign Relations Committee, and it was also a central theme in his essay "The Trivialization of Human Rights."[16] Lefever revealed no reservations about criticizing human rights violations and atrocities in the Soviet Union, Cuba, Cambodia, Vietnam, and North Korea. But the rhetoric of Patricia Derian, the first full-time Assistant Secretary of State for Human Rights and Humanitarian Affairs, was described as "moralistic rhetoric alien to traditional diplomatic discourse." President Carter's stance was seen as natural given his perspective as a "born-again Baptist and a latter-day Wilsonian."[17]

The critique of the Carter administration involved charges that it underestimated the danger of totalitarianism, overestimated American influence, mixed domestic and foreign policy concerns, ignored dangers of reform-intended intervention, overestimated the role of human rights in foreign policy, and was overly selective in its choice of human rights issues.

Lefever's blunt way of writing has led to his being misunderstood. His widely quoted suggestion that the United States had no responsibility to promote human rights was not meant as his last word on the subject. "In a formal and legal sense, the U.S. Government has no responsibility—and certainly no authority—to promote human rights in other sovereign states. But this is hardly the whole story."[18] He certainly argued that our domestic example of honoring human rights is an important example to the world. Also, the defense of allies who were threatened by totalitarian influences was the second major contribution the United States could make to promoting human rights. Seoul, Taipei, and Pretoria were seen as capitals where the practice of human rights was less than perfect but which should be defended in the name of peace and human rights and the criticism of violations of human rights softened. In his conclusion, he urged the president to "tone down his rhetoric," which was grounded in "a kind of vague, romantic optimism with an excessive confidence in the power of reason and goodwill."[19]

Lefever's target in Carter's rhetoric was particularly the president's commencement speech at Notre Dame in 1977. It is true that Lefever's remarks about the state of the world were more somber than President Carter's, but of the speeches of Carter on human rights this particular speech has many phrases that reflect the same Reinhold Niebuhr whom Lefever quoted in criticizing the administration.

> I believe we can have a foreign policy that is democratic, that is based on our fundamental values and that uses power and influence for humane purposes. Being confident of our own future, we are now free of that inordinate fear of Communism which once led us to embrace any dictator who joined us in our fear. For too many years we have been willing to adopt the flawed principles and tactics of our adversaries, sometimes abandoning our values for theirs. We fought fire with fire, never thinking that fire is better fought with water . . . . This does not mean that we can conduct our foreign policy by rigid moral maxims. We live in a world that is imperfect and will always be imperfect, a world that is complex and will always be complex. I understand fully the limits of moral suasion. I have no illusion that changes will come easily or soon. But I also believe that it is a mistake to undervalue the power of words and of the ideas that words embody.[20]

Carter was concerned to found the human rights issues as "a broad-based approach."[21] In his speeches he portrayed it not as a weapon aimed at the Soviet Union and its allies but as a reflection of the experience and ideals of the American people. He used the term *national interest*, but that term for him included the promotion of the ideals of the people. In his judgment the human rights issue was part of the ideological competition with the Soviet Union, but it was more than that. He argued that it necessarily had to be applied to allies and foes alike for it to maintain its credibility.

> We are determined in the United States to use our economic, social, political and military strength so we can never be successfully challenged by any competitive philosophy, and we are very eager to combine with our allies and friends to make sure this resolve is clearly undisputed by all. We have an eagerness to compete in an ideological way around the world, because we know that our commitment to human freedom, human rights and democratic principles, and our compassion toward the less fortunate than we will prevail. This is a commitment we want to share with you.[22]

Carter promised more than he could deliver in a foreign policy emphasizing human rights, but he conceded that human rights issues should not block progress on other issues like the control of nuclear weapons. He recognized the cold war, but he tried to downplay it, to create an attitude of détente. A major difference with Lefever is this refusal to make the clear-cut distinction between totalitarian and authoritarian nations concerning human rights policy. From a moral perspective, inattention to violations of human rights in Cambodia was a failure, and Lefever correctly criticized this blindness. Carter and Derian were certainly more forthright in criticizing allied human rights violations in the developing world. Andrew Young carried the human rights banner vis-à-vis Africa in a way that contradicted Lefever's judgments, but Lefever's judgments regarding Southern Africa were one of the items that resulted in senatorial critique in the hearing.

Carter was a complex person and his views on the relationship of morality to politics are deeper than his critics recognized. E. Brooks Holifield noted in Carter a rather Calvinist intraworldly asceticism in his evangelical Baptist tradition, an open American religiously pluralistic toleration, and a considerable amount of Christian realism.[23] And, indeed, Carter often remarked on his debt to Niebuhr. This debt to Niebuhr survives the detractions of those skeptical of the connection and is adequately defended in the arguments of June Bingham[24] and William Lee Miller.[25] Carter not only read and quoted Niebuhr, he understood politics as an expression of Christian social activism. He differed from Niebuhr in not forcefully criticizing the problems or even illusions of moral activism. It is just this critique of activism that characterized much of Lefever's writing and contributed to his defeat in the Senate Foreign Relations Committee. In a book of Niebuhr's essays, which Lefever had edited, Lefever left a clue to his own style:

> In fact one can perhaps best gain an understanding of Niebuhr's views on political morality by studying the criticism he makes of those persons who, in his view, misunderstand our moral responsibility as citizens and as a nation because they fail to understand the realities of politics.[26]

Ernest W. Lefever and Human Rights

It is much more difficult to ascertain Lefever's position on human rights than it is to understand either his mentor Reinhold Niebuhr or the object of his criticism, Jimmy Carter. Lefever's ambivalence on the application of human rights can perhaps be seen in three different periods: his critique of the Carter administration, his nomination to wear the human rights mantle, and finally his return to critiquing the United States emphasis on human rights in foreign policy.

In 1977 he downplayed the human rights policy as seen in the Carter administration.

> Making human rights the chief, or even major, foreign policy determinant carried dangers.
> 1. Giving human rights a central place subordinates, blurs, or distorts all other relevant considerations.[27]

In the winter of 1978, Lefever's lead sentence in his famous essay in *Policy Review* seemed to contradict this statement: "Human rights are what politics is all about."[28] However, the argument of the essay was essentially the same as that of the 1977 piece. Human rights was fundamentally a matter of protecting U.S. allies, and witnessing to the world a high standard of achievement in fulfilling human rights domestically. Several sentences deny the propriety of trying to enforce human rights through U.S. foreign policy.

Our President and all other heads of state have authority to act only in their own states, within the territory of their legal jurisdiction . . . .

In sum, U.S. aid can properly be given to encourage a friend or ally to pursue constructive external policies, but not to promote internal reforms opposed by the assisted government . . . .

In a formal and legal sense, the U.S. Government has no responsibility—and certainly no authority—to promote human rights in other sovereign states. . . . But this is hardly the whole story.[29]

He went on to emphasize the major contributions the U.S. could make to human rights by its example and the defense of peoples threatened by "totalitarian aggression or subversion."

On July 14, 1979, he testified before the Subcommittee on International Organizations of the House Foreign Affairs Committee that

in my view, the United States should remove from the statute books all clauses that establish a human rights standard or condition that must be met by another sovereign government before our government transacts normal business with it, unless specifically waived by the President.[30]

In the second stage of his involvement with human rights, as President Reagan's nominee for the Assistant Secretary of Human Rights position, he indicated that he regarded his former statement urging the removal of human rights standards from the law as a "goof." He tenaciously held to his commitment to participate in a review of such legislation under the new administration, but his earlier statement was regarded as too sweeping.

The hearings were long and the testimony from witnesses pro and con numerous. Significant issues of public policy and morality were debated. In the end the committee refused to recommend Lefever by a vote of 13 to 4. Different factors influenced various senators, but in their associating their views with those of Senator Percy and Senator Pell, those who gave their reasons for voting against him concurred that his public record on human rights in foreign policy was inadequate. His developed views would be an unfortunate symbol to the world. The American people still supported human rights and no signal that would encourage any harsh measures elsewhere should be given. His remarks about South Africa and Korea meant that his concern for human rights in those countries was not credible. His refusal to give an opinion on the Genocide Convention prevented him from appearing credible.[31]

Other important factors included a sense that he sublimated human rights concerns too easily to cold war considerations. He seemed not to understand the reasons why a Secretary for Human Rights needed to push the human rights issues forcefully even if U.S. foreign policy had to consider other factors also. Senator Percy also argued forcefully that the United States was stronger as a defender of democracy if it "spoke out for human rights across the board."[32] Many of the senators spoke of their willingness to support Lefever for other positions in government, but they opposed his public position on human rights for the United States government.

After the smoke of the battle over nomination had cleared, Lefever returned to developing the Ethics and Public Policy Center and to lecturing on human rights. His speech in Guam started like his *Policy Review* essay, but now politics was not *all* about human rights: "Human rights and security are what politics is all about."[33]

The close linking of human rights to the cold war dominated his presentation. An additional note was the rejection of the "so-called economic and social rights, such as the right to a job or health care."[34] They were to be regarded as objectives because only a totalitarian government could guarantee them. "The price of gaining these 'rights' is the sacrifice of freedom."[35] Societies like the United Kingdom or West Germany, which do guarantee health care, would be offended by that assumption. Rights of course are in part objectives and some societies achieve them better than others, and what some societies recognize as realities others only perceive as goals. The post-hearing lecture reaffirmed the Lefever the committee feared, and muted the Lefever who affirmed a more activist stance for human rights:

> The impulse to impose our standards or practice on other societies supported by policies of reward and punishment, leads inevitably to a kind of reform intervention. We Americans have no moral mandate to transform other societies, and we rightly resent such efforts on the part of totalitarians. There is more than a touch of arrogance in any efforts to alter the domestic behavior of allies or even of adversaries.[36]

Lefever as a person of conscience and conviction marches to his own drummer, and it was a different drummer from the one the Senate Committee heard. His own position may not have been understood by the committee for he did say on many occasions that the U.S. should use all appropriate means to defend or extend freedom. He argued for using one moral standard for totalitarian, authoritarian and democratic states. While recognizing that we could not even fulfill our own ideals, he urged a striving for Reinhold Niebuhr's "the relevance of an impossible ideal" to move the struggle for human rights further. The campaigns for him and against him both reached points not very interesting for this study.[37] The hearings and the reactions to them exhibited a lot of spiritual and moral pride and human fear.

The U.N. Human Rights Commission

Within two weeks of the inauguration of President Reagan, Michael Novak was seated as the U.S. representative to the Human Rights Commission. There had not been much time for briefing or background study. The positions expressed by Michael Novak and Richard Schifter, the alternative representative, were worked out on the spot in consultation with Washington. They found there that most of the participants did not agree on the meaning of human rights, they used language differently, and they differed in values. Novak also characterized the discussions as being full of lies, as exhibiting absurdity, and there being much double-talk.[38] The implication of Novak's remarks and the specific statement from his colleague was that the lack of agreement about human rights "makes the institution one from which no great positive contribution to the cause of human rights can be expected."[39]

The speeches of Schifter and Novak read like speeches of those who trust in their position, but who know they will lose the vote. The collection of their speeches and the relevant resolutions reveal they lost the votes.[40]

The U.S. delegation needed more flexibility. The United States was not alone at the session; other Western nations were there who share our traditions. A narrow definition of human rights that rejects attempts to relate human rights to economic development and disarmament is doomed to defeat. Human rights has its meaning in broad conceptions of conditions that will allow humanity to reach toward greater fulfillment. It cannot be confined to Western-style political institutions and to an apology for allies of the United States. It was a narrow conception of human rights and a too close connection of human rights with cold war politics that the senators rejected in Ernest Lefever. Our cold war politics will defend our interests, and we are not so weak that we have to insist that our imagination is limited to our own achievements in human rights. In the human rights debate we can afford to express our idealism. We can express our hopes for human rights in terms that elude our grasp and their immediate resolution. A narrow defense of our national interests appears cynical before the world. It must be mixed with idealism. The idealism of our own civil rights movement was mixed with realism in winning the civil rights victories in the country.

In our human rights spokespeople we need an expression of idealism that can agree with the hunger of the developing nations and with the idealism of many in our own country about the imperatives for international development and arms reduction. Christian realism at its best mixes the insights of the children of light with the wisdom of the children of darkness and does not insist that the only way to human rights is through our experience. In an earlier comment of my perspective on the tradition of Christian realism, Novak suggested it erred on the side of the children of light. Perhaps he was right, but certainly in our struggle for the human rights emphasis in our foreign policy, our spokespeople need to be reminded of the dangers of a realism that is too narrow. Let us express in our human rights positions a passion for reform even if in our full foreign policy that passion is compromised by our defense of our interests. We must run the risk of hypocrisy (since hypocrisy is the concession in which virtue acknowledges sin) rather than lose the human rights struggle.

The most comprehensive study to relate theological ethics to human rights finds the Reagan administration diminishing the accents of human rights in U.S. foreign policy.[41] Foreign policy regarding human rights is being conducted as if Lefever had been nominated. It is this passionate commitment to pursuing the cold war that blinds Michael Novak and others to the cruelty of this administration's policy. However, while the administration is tilting toward South Africa, the American population is becoming more activist in attacking apartheid in print and in the streets. While the administration continues to cover up human rights atrocities in Central America, polls show that the people refuse to support war in Central America to defend or restore inhumane regimes. Human rights becomes *practically* connected with peacemaking. The human rights legislation Lefever opposed becomes the chief legal restraint on the administration in pursuing war.

In 1986, some hoped for a shift in U.S. policy. The administration did not persist in defending Presidents Duvalier and Marcos but assisted them in departing when resistance became too great to their rule. Richard Schifter, who had become Assistant Secretary of State for Human Rights and Humanitarian Affairs, publically criticized Chile, admitting that Chile's responses to quiet diplomacy had been negligible. On the other hand, Elliot Abrahms, Schifter's predecessor, conducted the war policy in Central America using human rights as a weapon in the cold war. The World Court, however, ruled against the United States, finding it guilty in several instances of violating international law. Moreover, the United States was also found guilty of encouraging the Contras in actions that violated humanitarian law.

The Reagan administration seems to have followed its own rhetoric: It uses human rights to criticize Communist enemies, but is incapable of guiding its policies toward anti-Communist allies by human rights standards. Right-wing religious forces repeat Amaziah's mistake of thinking human rights concerns are not to be heard in the administration's precincts. Consequently, refusing to end support for oppression or to criticize injustice in anti-Communist forces, a great nation lurches along, violating the sensitivities of much of the world and violating minimal standards of justice.

Human rights are easily subject to abuse in foreign policy. Both the idealist and the cynic misuse them. Only a policy that recognizes their foundations in human nature itself, notes that historically they are realized only fragmentarily through struggle, and possesses a hope for their ever-expanded fulfillment can negotiate between idealistic moralism and political amoralism.

V. THE JUSTIFIABLE WAR TRADITION

The perspective taken on the tradition of the justifiable war is crucial. It is of central concern that the tradition be examined in light of an ethic of the just peace. For the Christian life, the ethic of the just peace ought to predominate. Consideration of questions of the justice of particular wars or justified participation in a particular war is a secondary part of any adequate Christian ethic. Even after all that it has been possible to do for peace has been undertaken, the morally sensitive Christian will be confronted by the question of whether a particular struggle involving armed forces can be entered. The justifiable war tradition itself has this requirement: For a war to be accepted, it must be a matter of last resort. We live in a world besieged by war and rumors of war, a world predisposed to war. The most peaceful nation will be confronted by the question of engaging or refusing to engage in wars in which issues vital to its well-being are involved. The Christian individual cannot escape reasoning about the morality of particular conflicts that impinge on life, family, and community. Even if we were to achieve an international order that would reduce the current international anarchy, decisions about threats to that order would still have to use moral criteria about the just or unjust use of military force.

Those who are seeking the peace of God still live in a world in which war is to be expected. Particular wars can be avoided and international conflicts are often resolved without war. The twentieth century is characterized by war, and even the most peaceful have to think about the reality of war. Those who try to achieve peace after the style of the Romans and who mix the use of force with diplomacy also have to think about justifying war. Christians who want to be politically responsible, while seeking to make war less likely, must also be able to reason about each potential conflict while holding that reason within a Christian theological perspective.

The justifiable war tradition is not primarily an issue of biblical ethics. The wars of Israel are seen in the perspective of God controlling the affairs of humanity, and they seldom rise to the perception of human beings reasoning about the appropriateness of war. The hunger for peace is a major motif of biblical faith, but the role of humans acting as agents to achieve that peace or to prevent war is not often acknowledged. Jesus resisted the appeals to force and did not adopt the Zealot option of resisting Rome by force. His early followers sought to participate in God's peace, but they did not actively try to formulate state policy. Despite the blessing of the peacemakers, the avoidance of Zealotry, and the ethic of nonresistance, Jesus does not unequivocally provide advice about how his followers are to live regarding conflict between states. He was realistic in expecting violence, but he did not provide guidance for how his followers would direct a state. The historical probability is that he anticipated the end of history and God's complete victory as more imminent than the possibility of his followers succeeding to power in Rome. These earlier followers of Jesus addressed in the New Testament were a relatively separatist, sectarian movement without political power.

The first three centuries of the Christian era found Christians opposing war, though some soldiers were converted to Christianity. Disarmament was not a requirement of conversion. By the end of the second century, Christians were in the armies and many Christians were witnessing that the Christian way was that of nonviolence. From the end of the second century until the time of Constantine in the beginning of the fourth century, the evidence of Christian presence in the armies increases while the voices of the major theologians oppose Christians taking human life in war.

Augustine of Hippo

The situation changed with Constantine's victory over his foes. Constantine favored Christianity and used it as a civil religion to cement together the torn fabric of the empire. On his deathbed he was baptized and in his life he turned the empire toward the faith he adopted. Given its growing civil status, Christianity began to adjust to its imperial prerogatives. Ambrose, the spiritual father of Augustine, used the just-war teaching of Cicero to justify the Christian use of force in defensive wars. Augustine himself was to give to Christian thought the outlines of a position justifying the use of armed force. His reflections shaped Christian morals on the issue and laid the groundwork for both the Roman Catholic theory in Thomas Aquinas and in Protestantism in the thought of John Calvin and Martin Luther.

Augustine (354–430) lived in an age of war and plunder and none of his writing glorifies war. He had a great aversion to war and scorn for those who gloried in it. War originated in sin and it was not to be praised. His major work, *The City of God*, elaborated the search for peace and the peace of God. Peace was the aim of all peoples, but few found it and the peace achieved in the earthly realm was usually only an armed truce. The Roman Empire's peace, even in its successful years of the past, had led to civil and social wars.

In a letter to Boniface, the Count of Africa, he censored the personal morals of Boniface and reminded him of his spiritual destiny. He instructed him to "Love the Lord thy God with all thy strength: and love thy neighbor as thyself." He reminded Boniface that in a personal conversation he had urged Boniface not to retire to a monastery, but to fulfill his earthly responsibilities. He praised his earlier work as a military commander when he had defended Africa against the invaders. He urged him, now, to secure the peace so that Africa could live in harmony. He urged on him the necessity of ordering his commanders so that the aggressors could be defeated and peace be secured. As he wrote elsewhere he advised him: "Therefore even in waging war, cherish the spirit of a peacemaker, that by conquering those whom you attack, you may lead them back to the advantage of peace; for our Lord says: 'Blessed are the peacemakers; for they shall be called children of God.' "[1] The urgings of Augustine on his friend to stem the "African barbarians" did not bring an end to the wars, or peace to Africa. Shortly after Augustine's death, his own city of Hippo was devastated. His testimony to Boniface reflects the insight of Augustine that wars in defense of people and the order of the state could be morally defended.

The goal of any justifiable war is still peace. Peace is the great goal of humanity, and the inner desire to achieve peace must be the aim of any war. This is the appropriate presupposition for all Christian thinking about war. Peace, not just a Roman peace or a truce, reflecting the deep Old Testament longing for fullness of life and the

New Testament sense of peace as a blessing, is the goal. Peace as the harmony among people is the theme of Augustine's great philosophy of history in *The City of God*, and it points to a fullness of the meaning of peace similar to the definition of justice in Plato's *Republic*.

A war—to be rightly engaged in—must vindicate justice. This is not to imply perfection in history, but certainly it excludes wars of selfish conquest or illegal wars. In Augustine's thought it is close to the first requirement that the intention is peace. It must accomplish peace or harmony among people rather than contribute to disharmony, discord, and further wars.

The disposition of those engaged in the war must be love. Augustine's neoplatonism could permit him to devalue the body and be fairly casual about the possibility of loving the one whom one slays. Yet the requirement of love stands as a testimony against the hatred that usually accompanies war. It distinguishes thought about a justifiable war from fanatical crusades in which love of the enemy is rejected. The love ethic that dominates Augustine's thought enjoins him in the direction of responsibility for those who cannot protect themselves. Boniface would have retired from public life, but in this world Christians are obligated to fulfill their roles as public citizens to protect order—even though disorder is contained within the public institutions. The love is also obligatory toward those one opposes in war.

It is this requirement to protect the innocent through the agencies of public order that underlies the further requirements of a justified war. It must be carried out by those responsible for public order. Love is expressed through the ambiguous institutions of the state as they properly fulfill their responsibility to protect the citizens. Only much later in Christian history, after ideas of the sovereignty of the people had been accepted, could the idea of a justified war be transmitted into a justified revolution.

Roland H. Bainton in drawing on the studies of Gustave Combes understands Augustine to require also the conduct of war be subject to moral rules.[2] The rules were drawn from classical sources and they prohibited massacre, looting, looting temples, atrocities, and so forth, and require that dealing with the enemy be honest. Augustine saw the very barbarians who were invading Rome as demonstrating the influence of Christianity in their attempts to humanize war.

For Augustine, Christians would only participate in war in their official capacities in government or in the army. The private citizen had no right to take the sword even in self-defense. Clergy and monks because of their religious vocation were excluded from war. The monks were to seek perfection, and their obligations forbade participation in war as it excluded them from marriage or property.

Augustine's ethic clearly excluded most wars from the recognition of justified warfare. War was a horrible evil and the Christian was more to be praised for avoiding war through negotiation than for engaging in a war—even if it *was* justifiable.[3] Basically, only wars of defense or to right an objective wrong could be justified. Even when justified, the Christian could engage in war *only* with a sorrowful mind.

Augustine's position, in summary, was that of an ethic of love thinking about difficult choices in a sinful warring world. He used insights from scripture, classical philosophy, and the history of the world, but he transformed these insights through the ethic of love to promote peace. The openness to some participation in war, combined, however, with political responsibility, could lead others less rigorous in their commitment to peace to rationalize participating in wars that Augustine would have regarded as unjustified.

Augustine's influence continued in church circles, but the influence of his just-war tradition was minimal.[4] Popes used his political ideas in their own way, and the major center of Christian civilization of Byzantium was relatively free of Augustine's influence. The church tried to restrain war through the Truce of God and the Peace of God. Gradually some merging of the spirit of the conquerors and the teaching of the church emerged in the rules of chivalry. The wars of the Crusades were of a spirit quite contrary to the just-war tradition and the Crusading Religious War emerged as a third option in the Christian ethic of war.

In the twelfth century, Roman law was revived by Gratian's canon law. Augustine was the major source on the ethics of war in Gratian's codification of law, the *Decretum*. James T. Johnson locates the origin of the medieval theory of just war with Gratian and his successors in canon law.[5]

Thomas Aquinas

Augustine had written at a time of the destruction of civilization. Thomas Aquinas (1225–1274) wrote at a time of the rebuilding of civilization. He is portrayed as calm with a book in his hands. The Crusades were not yet defeated; religious extremism, papal schism, and the Black Death were in the future. Political institutions, law, universities, cathedrals, and business were being developed. It was a mediating time, and Thomas's great work was to mediate the newly discovered Aristotelian philosophy into Augustinian theology.

He did not criticize the Crusades, in fact inasmuch as they had been to defend rights of Christians in pagan lands, he approved of them. His own noble family, the Aquino, suffered under war. He himself chose the contemplative life and did not become, in his writing, a party to the struggles of his day. He turned down the proffered Archbishopric of Naples, which his family wanted for him, and continued his teaching and writing.

His writing on war is brief. He draws on Augustine to support the conclusions about war drawn from natural law. The natural law is the inclination to good, which corresponds to human rational nature. The teaching on justifiable war is in his most sustained treatise on political philosophy within the *Summa Theologica*. The natural law participates in the eternal law of God's mind; it is the way rational creatures reflect God's law.

Thomas presupposed some unity in Western Europe, even though Christian Spain was fighting to drive out the Moslems, internal wars among Christian princes continued, and neither the emperor nor the pope could effectively govern. City-states were emerging and in England and France the foundations of the nation-state were slowly taking shape. The empire was beginning to come undone, but still there was sufficient unity to articulate a universal ethic based on rational principles. His thought still undergirds Roman Catholic thought on war and is foundational to the pastoral letter of the U.S. bishops. Protestant theologians used his thought to reinforce their rejection of American participation in the Vietnam war. Aquinas listed the principles in a systematic way, but such a listing cannot obscure his own sense of a universe full of people conjoined both to evil and good. Through the agency of ordered life, the good in humanity could order and contain the evil, thus expressing more fully God's intention. Part of the good ordering of the human community was the need for the defense of the common good against assaults by the enemy, even through the resort to war.

In the *Summa Theologica*, Thomas put his views succinctly:

1. The war must be declared by the competent ruler who has the duty to defend the state.

2. There must be a just cause for the war. (He quotes from Augustine to the point that the war is to correct a wrong.)
3. There must be "a right intention on the part of the belligerents." The desire to hurt, the thirst for power, the cruel vendetta are all condemned.[6]

This thought of Aquinas has been expanded in various ways by other moral theorists. Joseph C. McKenna has expounded Roman Catholic just-war thought in seven principles:

1. Legitimate authority declares and executes the war.
2. The injury which the war is intended to prevent must be a real injury (not a fiction).
3. The seriousness of the injury to be prevented must be proportionate to the destructiveness of the war.
4. There must be a reasonable hope of success. (McKenna: "Defensive war may be hopeless, but offensive war must contain elements of success.") Pope Pious XII ruled out offensive war as an instrument of policy. No movement across boundaries can be justified.
5. War must be engaged in only as a last resort.
6. The intention of entering into the war must be just.
7. The measures used in conducting war must be defensible. Preservation of non-combatants has always been a factor in the question of a just war.[7]

John Calvin

John Calvin (1509–1564) continued the Augustinian tradition. In his exposition of the sixth commandment "You shall not kill," killing means murder. He deepens the commandment to exclude hatred. The neighbor is to be held sacred. "If you wish or plan anything contrary to the safety of a neighbor, you are considered guilty of murder." Intent to do harm is condemned, even murder of the heart is forbidden, for God looks upon the thought as well as actions. However, this strong teaching also enjoins responsibility:

> We are accordingly commanded, if we find anything of use to us in saving our neighbor's lives faithfully to employ it; if there is anything that makes for their peace to see to it; if anything harmful to ward it off; if they are in any danger to lend a helping hand.[8]

This responsibility to prevent harm means that the magistrates must defend their people. The responsibilities of the rulers to punish wrongdoers for the public's protection extended to the ruler's responsibility to protect their territory from invasion. His reference to the rule of natural justice is to defensive war *only*. He believed that the Old Testament declared such defensive wars to be lawful and the New Testament contained no rules against the lawfulness of such wars to Christians. He urged all the rulers to be very cautious in regard to war. All other means should be tried first. Wars were not to become excuses for the fulfillment of one's own passions. Following Plato he argued that the object of war must be peace.[9] On this right of defensive war followed the appropriateness of garrisons, alliances, and the possession of civil munitions, that is, the means to defend the territory. The alliances he mentions as appropriate are also defensive in character. The needs of Geneva, a small city-state, were well served by the factors Calvin mentioned. His ministry would include the strengthening of the city's defenses and defensive alliances.

Application to Our Time

Obviously, the defense of the American empire is a long way from the defense of Geneva. The Presbyterian Church, however, as recently as 1969 advocated the just-war tradition as a way of thinking about issues of Christian participation in war. The tradition was their individual participation or refusal to participate in war. The General Assembly quoted from a Presbyterian ethicist's book, affirming six principles as representative criteria:

1. All other means to the morally just solution of a conflict must be exhausted before resort to arms can be regarded as legitimate.
2. War can be just only if employed to defend a stable order or morally preferable cause against threats of destruction or the rise of injustice.
3. Such a war must be carried out with the right attitudes.
4. A just war must be explicitly declared by a legitimate authority.
5. A just war may be conducted only by military means that promise a reasonable attainment of the moral and political objectives being sought.
6. The just war theory has also entailed selective immunity for certain parts of the population, particularly for non-combatants.[10]

Such guidelines, whether regarded as rational reflection on the natural order as Augustine taught or as principles of a natural law as

Thomas thought or as a distillation of the moral tradition of the Western world as Michael Walzer uses them, are to be used as we consider just war.

They do permit limited uses of military force in defensive wars. They clearly prohibit massive bombing of population centers as exercised in World War II and the Vietnam conflict. They rule out wars of aggression and wars to gain political influence over another country or for cold war advantage. They can, if amended, be used to justify some wars of revolution against governments that oppress their people. For Christians who regard the defense of the innocent from loss of their lives or liberties as an action to be taken sorrowfully out of responsibility, they provide a means of moral reasoning.

These criteria clearly regard any wars illegitimate that are conducted for selfish national interest calculations. Most wars that characterize our warring planet should be regarded as immoral by Christians, using these criteria. Weapons of mass destruction, whether biological or chemical or nuclear, are clearly unable to be used under the absolute prohibition of protecting the lives of noncombatants. These weapons cannot be limited in their destruction to legitimate military targets except for a few highly unlikely uses of the weapons. The targeting of these weapons on available military targets, at the present time, involves intending to murder millions of citizens—including millions of children and other noncombatants. Such weapons mean that the war cannot be a responsible act of self-protection. The available evidence regarding nuclear war points to unacceptable levels of ecological destruction, and the possible end of human history.

Ethics based on Christian realism permits limited use of deadly force to officers defending themselves and others in society. It does not permit police officers to destroy an apartment house full of people to stop the illegal activity of a criminal. The analogy applies to war: Some use of deadly force by the appropriate officers of a state is permitted, but Christian ethics does not permit the destruction of an enemy nation's people, even in the defense of others.

Christian ethics is not only an ethic of means and ends, it is also an ethic of intention. Jesus was concerned about the immortality of the person's mind, as well as the immorality of the person's actions. It is immoral to intend to do evil. Therefore, we cannot intend to destroy a nation's children, even if that nation attacks ours. We cannot morally tolerate a policy that threatens the children of a rival power.

Deterrence fails not because it may not work, but because it is itself an evil intention. Thus, under the conditions of some modern wars, Christians arguing over the ethics of responsible love in just-war reasoning will be led to nuclear pacifism. When they focus on the intention of deterrent policy, which will under certain conditions destroy the other nation's people, they will reject it. To reject the deterrence of nuclear holocaust is not to reject deterrence by means of legitimate deployment of armed forces.

The policy of deterrence and intended use of nuclear weapons fails by several other criteria of the justified use of military force. Reference to the criteria of the 1969 General Assembly makes this clear:

1. It has led to actions that thwart the search for just solutions to the conflict between the superpowers. Our diplomacy is characterized by a lack of imaginative solutions to the issues dividing the superpowers. The installation of the new missile system for the sake of the capacity to increase our war-fighting capacity has resulted in the increase of bellicosity between the superpowers.
2. Nuclear war cannot be carried out with right attitudes. Present plans for a limited counterforce exchange identify sixty military targets in or near Moscow. The U.S.S.R. has repeatedly stated that a nuclear war will not be limited, but that it will result in the complete destruction of both societies.
3. The second criterion could conceivably be fulfilled.
4. No authority has the legitimate right to practice genocide or omnicide. Such warfare is a crime against humanity and against God's authority.
5. Nuclear war is not carried out by military means appropriate to the moral and political objectives being sought. Nuclear war is an act of madness.
6. Selective immunity for noncombatants is violated in the planning for nuclear war.

The moral rejection of contemporary war plans and deterrence strategy suggests a change in direction. The churches need to make their moral judgments clear. Practical adjustments can follow moral clarity. The ethics of ambiguity, which allowed the churches to denounce nuclear buildup while accepting nuclear deterrence, needs to be overcome. The acceptance of nuclear deterrence tended to legitimate the buildup to today's more than 60,000 nuclear weapons.

Does moral clarity require unilateral, nuclear disarmament? No! Complete nuclear disarmament will probably never happen. Unilateral disarmament is only feasible after military threats are removed. The diagnosis of an illness does not mean that suicidal or silly therapies should be adopted. Some unilateral steps can be taken. Both NATO and the Warsaw Pact have practiced some unilateral disarmament. Neither side practices complete military preparedness. But significant reductions in weapons of mass destruction will have to be negotiated. Agreements will need to be mutual. For a mixture of moral, economic, and prudent measures, the Soviet Union and the United States will have to work out their security through negotiated disarmament. Progress on political disagreements will need to accompany the disarmament plan. A goal of complete, general disarmament is utopian. A goal of radical reduction in weapons of mass destruction between the superpowers is realistic. The guarantees of the peace will reside in our radical reduction of the terror, our success in cooperating to reduce the terror, and the gradual turning of détente into mutuality between nations.

The real seizing of the opportunity for superpower disarmament will make possible the strengthening of the nonproliferation policies, which are in the interests of the whole world as well as the superpowers.

The Catholic Bishops

The pastoral letter of the U.S. bishops on war and peace, *The Challenge of Peace: God's Promise and Our Response,* which used just-war criteria, arrived at a slightly different position. They were led to "a strictly conditional moral acceptance of nuclear deterrence. We cannot consider it adequate as a long term basis for peace." They then moved on with several suggestions for moving beyond deterrence. They also said that they could not approve of every system of weapons or policy designed to strengthen deterrence. It is impossible to reconcile the just-war criteria with approval of the present system of deterrence or with the plans for installing the Strategic Defense Initiative system to defend land-based missiles. The same moral arguments render morally unacceptable the development of Russian, Chinese, French, and British arsenals of mass destruction. The intention of nuclear war is wrong—even if it is a response to the failure of deterrence. The bishops' willingness to reconsider their position points toward the weakness of their moral acceptance of nuclear deterrence.

The French bishops' meeting at Lourdes issued a statement on "Winning Peace" on November 8, 1983. It is a rigorous, imaginative statement by the bishops of a country with its own nuclear deterrent. The bishops admit that their deterrent, wherein the strong are deterred by the weak, is an anti-city strategy. Still, they insist that the threat to use nuclear weapons must not be treated morally the same as the actual use of the weapons. "Threat is not use." With the German bishops, they argue that "Charity cannot replace right." They recognize two evils: capitulation or counterthreat. They think counterthreat is morally acceptable if it meets certain conditions:

— It must concern defensive exclusively;
— Overarmament is avoided: deterrence is attained the moment the formulated threat renders aggression by a third party senseless;
— Every precaution is taken to avoid "an error" or the intervention of a demented person, a terrorist, etc.;
— The nation taking the risk of nuclear deterrence adheres to a constructive policy in favor of peace. [11]

The French bishop statement fails logically because they see but two options: capitulation or counterthreat. They are led by the position of their church and government to support grudgingly counterthreat, and to distinguish threat from use. The willingness to use, however, is necessary to threat, and one cannot intend to do evil. There are other options: Diplomacy, negotiation, and the building of mutual interdependence between the Soviet Union and Europe are the most obvious examples. The bishops want diplomacy and negotiation; firm church opposition to the intent to use these weapons would encourage the nations to act reasonably.

The United Methodist Bishops, 1986

The Council of Bishops of The United Methodist Church in 1986 affirmed the continuing relevance of both the pacifist and the just-war traditions. They were careful to set their study of the just-war tradition within the confines of recommended principles for a just peace. They respectfully noted that the Catholic bishops' Pastoral Letter of 1983 and the General Convention of the Episcopal Church of 1982 had both affirmed a policy of nuclear deterrence with qualifications. Their own finding was that nuclear deterrence as well as any use of nuclear weapons was morally untenable. Their analysis led them to affirm the just-war tradition and to say "A clear and unconditional No, to nuclear war and to any use of nuclear weapons."[12]

The paper of the bishops is under study and discussion in The United Methodist Church. Within the spectrum developed in the paper of possible positions on the morality of war, the bishops have affirmed a nuclear pacifist position of no nuclear deterrence or use. This action by the leadership of the second largest Protestant denomination is significant. It will encourage other denominations to push the increasing moral rejection of nuclear weapons. As government policy has moved toward preparing to fight a nuclear war and justifying this preparation as strengthening a deterrent, church thinking, represented by the United Methodist bishops, is rejecting nuclear deterrence itself.

The Strategic Defense Initiative

Ironically, the recognition is growing that nuclear deterrence promotes nuclear holocaust in response to certain possible historical actions; for example the unlikely but possible invasion of Europe has encouraged the development of more weapons. Recognizing the dangers and immorality in nuclear war, President Reagan has called for a policy of high-technology defense. Despite resistance in the scientific community and doubts among Congressional leaders, the research is being funded at more than four billion dollars annually. The boost to the high-technology sector of the arms race, in which American leadership is clear, has caused anxiety among Soviet leaders. They have responded with a variety of arms control and disarmament initiatives related to limiting space-based weapons.

On the face of it, proposals to further militarize space do not seem to increase security or promote peace. Is there something in the "Star Wars" proposals that is not obvious? In the announcements to advance research in the area of space-based weapons, the administration originally talked of a protective shield. The emphasis was on defensive weapons rather than offensive weapons. Plausibly defensive weapons could relate to a moral tradition like justifiable war thinking.

Investigation and the elaboration of plans soon revealed that no shield was possible or projected. Rather a vast array of ground-based and space-based weapons was intended. The ground-based weapons systems were probably not offensive weapons and their chief danger was in weakening the antiballistic missile treaty, which is one of the few arms-limiting agreements still in force. It is relatively impossible to distinguish between defensive and offensive weapons based in space. As an offensive weapon or as a defensive weapon, a laser or a rail gun in orbit is potentially dangerous. Both are potential offensive weapons against satellites or earth-bound targets. The Star Wars plans promise no shield, only more high-technology swords.

More ominously, the law projected that the potential-kill ratio of a space-based defense system makes it of little use in defending the United States against a Soviet first strike. It sends a signal to the Soviet Union that its potential as a follow-up step against the Soviet Union after a United States first strike is a more efficient use of the system. Again, U.S. policy is largely read as preparing to fight the nuclear war and not by waiting until the United States has suffered the first blow. So the Star Wars scenarios increase Soviet anxieties, which are already high, and spread false hopes in the United States of technological fixes to political and spiritual problems. In light of these considerations, the Star Wars addition to the present nuclear policies does not move these policies closer to meeting the justifiable war traditions.

The fascination with the future possibilities of a defense against ICBMs has led the administration of President Reagan into questioning the treaty of 1972 regarding limiting antiballistic missile defense. The abandoning of SALT II has taken the limits off the number of nuclear weapons delivery vehicles and opened the Pandora's box of unlimited development of new delivery vehicles. Such a development makes the possibility of a Star Wars defense even less likely than its earlier critics suspected.[13]

The moral defense of adding a Star Wars defense to expanding numbers of nuclear weapons delivery systems has focused on the desirability of defense over offensive use of nuclear weapons. In Kenneth W. Kemp's defense of Star Wars, he has quoted President Reagan himself regarding retaliation as being immoral.[14]

> Think of it. You're sitting at that desk. The word comes that they [the missiles] are on their way . . . . Your only response can be to push the button before they get here so that even though you're all going to die, they're going to die too . . . . There's something so immoral about it.[15]

Captain Kemp of the Air Force Academy then argues that the Strategic Defense Initiative gives another option. This type of argument is a reaching for a technological fix to a political and a human problem. The solution to the immoral position of nuclear weapons is not to advance toward the militarization of outer space. It is to recognize the shared responsibility of the United States and the Soviet Union with the cooperation of other powers to work diplomatically to reduce the nuclear terror. Deterrence interferes with diplomacy by forcing terror upon the diplomatic process. Solutions lie in the direction of recognizing a shared fate, stopping further development, mutual reduction of weaponry, working always for a shared greater stability in weaponry, developing nuclear-free zones, and building policies and armaments together toward no first use of weapons of mass destruction. These policies require changed perceptions of both superpowers toward each other, which can only be achieved by a rush toward understanding and give-and-take in negotiations.

The argument that the Strategic Defense Initiative of President Reagan is unwise means that its discontinuation should be negotiated with the Soviet Union along with the discontinuation of their work on advanced weapons for antiballistic missile defense. Strict treaties forbidding the testing of weapons in space are urgently needed to put a cap on the awesome new possibilities. Both the Soviet Union and the United States have been engaged in research for exotic new weapons for defense and domination in outer space. The President's SDI emphasis has contributed to making the issues public and in accelerating the U.S. program. A corresponding Soviet acceleration is possible.[16]

The just-war criteria, which are a way of thinking about permissible Christian use of violence for defense, are helpful guidelines for many of the conflicts that take place in the modern world. Counterterrorist policies, for example, need to be regulated by the just-war tradition's insistence on both just cause and just means. The modern weapons of mass destruction fall outside the permissible use of violence by Christians. Biological and chemical weapons carry inherently within themselves grave risks to noncombatant populations, which just-war thinking protects. Nuclear weapons have taken on the characteristics of suicide for the human race. Jonathan Schell's *The Fate of the Earth* summarizes and synthesizes the scientific evidence to show that nuclear exchanges among the nuclear powers could destroy human life. The research reported by Carl Sagan asserted the high probability that even a controlled nuclear war of 500 to 2,000 explosions of strategic warheads would create a catastrophe threatening to destroy humanity.[17] Sagan referred to his groups' findings by way of the science fiction terminology of the Doomsday machine. We have created, unrestrained by just-war criteria, means of war which, if used, threaten to kill us all. Some of the authors of the 1983 study made popular by Sagan moderated their claims in 1986 on the basis of new calculations. In particular they tended to project less temperature change owing to a limited nuclear exchange, but the stressed dangers to biological systems remained as great as ever.[18]

Obviously we know it is wrong to intend actions that threaten all of humanity. This conclusion can be reached without the just-war tradition. No Christian ethics can rightly argue for nuclear war. Christian ethics must also consider the intent of our planning. We must cherish the neighbor as made in the image of God and in our own flesh. As Calvin said,

> He who has merely refrained from shedding blood has not therefore avoided the crime of murder. If you perpetrate anything by deed, if you plot anything by attempt, if you wish or plan anything contrary to the safety of a neighbor, you are considered guilty of murder.[19]

Christian ethics, when it permits the killing of another human being, does so only under highly restricted conditions. Wars of defense and wars of revolution may occasionally meet these restrictions; nuclear war cannot. We have the just-war tradition and its insight in terms of what it is sometimes permissible to do to protect our neighbor. This tradition regarding weapons of mass destruction is clear: They are morally intolerable. If a government over a long period of time is threatening the survival of humanity on the planet, it begins to lose its legitimacy. Governments are constituted to restrain sin, to promote order, to secure for their people life and liberty. If their constituted regular policies are to plan a nuclear apocalypse under certain circumstances, they need to be changed. Four decades into the nuclear age, we are beginning to see the necessity and the difficulty of transforming our government to fit the reality.

VI. REVOLUTION AND COUNTERREVOLUTION IN CENTRAL AMERICA

Is revolutionary war in Central America morally justified? The foregoing chapter presupposes that there are situations in which the recourse to war is justifiable. *Justifiable* means that under certain conditions it is morally better to fight the war than to desist from fighting. Such situations are basically of three kinds. In each type war is already being inflicted and the recourse to war is to seek a just peace. First, a war may be justifiable if it is a defensive war. Second, a war of intervention to save a people from destruction or particularly grievous violations of human rights may be justifiable. Third, a revolutionary war to release a people from the ravages of a government that is particularly oppressive may be justifiable. In the second and third types one would argue that wars of intervention or revolution are essentially defensive wars to restore peace. Each of the three types would have to meet the generally recognized principles of justifiable war to make a moral case for their prosecution. People will disagree about whether particular wars meet the criteria and on the particular formulation of the criteria for revolutionary wars.[1] However, in a world in which both absolute pacifism and surrendering all decisions to the state are morally irresponsible, we must reason with standards of justifiable war or similar standards.

When, as Christians, we are citizens of either revolutionary countries or counterrevolutionary countries, our questions of the morality of revolution address our theological traditions. Our theological tradition has generally been reluctant to endorse revolution. The tradition since Constantine has been so subservient to Caesar that revolutionary theology has been a minor theme. Major exceptions to the subduing of revolutionary motifs are found in Gregory VII in the eleventh century, in the Reformation in the sixteenth century, in different ways in Martin Luther, in the Peasants' rebellion, and in the revolutionary followers of Calvin.[2] Christian revolutionaries carried out two of the world's most successful revolutions—in England in the seventeenth century and the American Revolution in the late eighteenth century. If the threat of modernism and radical socialism led the churches into reaction in the nineteenth century, the twentieth century saw Sun Yatsen leading the revolution in China and Christian participation in the worldwide decolonization of the postwar period. In India and the United States, the British and the American legal structures proved themselves vulnerable and responsive to massive religious civil disobedience led by Gandhi and King, which resisted the violence usually associated with revolution.

Ambiguity and Antirevolution

Still the theological tradition has been reluctant to endorse revolution. The reluctance is grounded, of course, in Christian institutional self-interest but also in a valuable insight. The insight is that historical life contains only ambiguous fulfillments. Revolutionary romanticism may promise that which is historically impossible and produce mostly death and destruction. Paul Tillich participated in a revolution in 1918, lost one in 1933, observed many, and reflected on revolution in his *Systematic Theology*.

> There are situations in which only a revolution (not always a bloody one) can achieve the breakthrough to a new creation. Such violent breakthroughs are examples of destruction for the sake of creation, a destruction sometimes so radical that a new creation becomes impossible and a slow reduction of the group and its culture to the stage of almost vegetative existence takes place. It is this danger of utter chaos that gives the established powers the ideological justification to suppress revolutionary forces or to try to overcome them in a counterrevolution.[3]

Paul the apostle's rejection of eschatological enthusiasts in Romans 13 is not directed against solid revolutionary movements. Theology has to reject both blind defense of injustice and enthusiastic dreams of absolute justice to allow the truly creative to appear. Tillich rejects the antirevolutionary bias of much of the tradition.

The principal antirevolutionary attitude of many Christian groups is fundamentally wrong, whether unbloody culture or unbloody and bloody political revolutions are concerned. The chaos which follows any kind of revolution can be a creative chaos. If history-bearing groups are unwilling to take this risk and are successful in avoiding any revolution, even an unbloody one, the dynamics of history will leave them behind.[4]

The revolutionary tradition of my own church, the Presbyterian Church (U.S.A.), has been most forcefully expressed in Calvinist, religious revolutionary movements in Switzerland, France, the Netherlands, England, Scotland, and North America. Since the end of the eighteenth century, however, Calvinist have not generally been though of as revolutionary. Their politics have been expressed within the parliamentary bodies of their countries and have generally contributed a sense of responsibility within liberal-political processes. In the United States, Presbyterian attitudes toward revolution are represented by James Madison's respect for structured change rather than Thomas Jefferson's enthusiasm for a revolution every so often.

So the revolutions of Central America pose difficult questions for the religious establishment of the United States. In fact the revolutionary movements of Central America often are perceived as a threat to U.S. interests. U.S. interests and the tendency of much of American religion to express the antirevolutionary tendency Tillich criticized pose a heavy threat to the possibility of revolutionary success in Central America. The United States has been invading Central America for more than a century. Often these invasions have been given moral and religious grounds. Recently these invasions have taken on an anti-Communist ideological cover, which is often part of a religious worldview. The 1954 overthrow of the Arbenz government in Guatemala, for example, was engineered by Allen Dulles as Director of the C.I.A. and overseen by John Foster Dulles as Eisenhower's Secretary of State. John F. Dulles' anti-Communism was integrated with his rigid, lawyerlike Presbyterianism. In fact, his work for the Federal Council of Churches' Commission for a Just and Durable Peace kept him in the public limelight. Peace in his religious anti-Communism meant the maintenance of non-Communist order in the American sphere of influence. Early in his career his mind had displayed an openness to change, but the integration of his faith and anti-Communism blinded him to the possibility of reform movements with leftist leanings in Latin America. Perhaps even more to the point than the anti-Communism or legalistic Presbyterianism of the Dulles brothers were their connections with the United Fruit Company, whose dominant landholdings in Guatemala were threatened with nationalization under the Arbenz government. Real economic interests are now closely related to anti-Communism. However, since the invasions of Central America by North Americans predate our Civil War, it is impossible to regard them all as motivated by anti–Russian communism sentiments. North American invasions of Central America over the last century are common; the interjection of anti-Russian influence is a recently offered justification. Status quo powers generally try to suppress revolutionary movements that threaten the regional arrangements. The United States has used the threat of chaos, the threat to American nationals, the threat to monetary stability, and now the threat to regional security to rationalize its invasions. Beneath all of these rationalizations is the perception of the interest of the U.S. business community. The interests of the business community are not self-sufficient explana tions, but they may not be ignored in U.S. foreign policy toward Central America.

Nicaragua and El Salvador

The Reagan administration is confronted in Nicaragua with a leftist-coalition regime that is popular. The regime is opposed by sectors of the Roman Catholic Church, including the Roman Curia; it is supported by the people's church and many of the Protestant churches.[5] It tolerates some dissent, and it conducted elections in 1984 which, under the semiwar conditions in which they were conducted, were generally regarded as quite fair. This revolutionary government representing many sectors of society is perceived as a threat to the unpopular governments of El Salvador, Honduras, and Guatemala. El Salvador and Guatemala face insurgencies and counterinsurgency governmental terror. The countries share a region that originally was the Central American Republic; they share poverty, culture, Catholicism, the Spanish language, and political immaturity. The Reagan policy was to support former soldiers of Somoza and other dissidents from Nicaragua to overthrow the Sandinista government. Congress disagreed at first and until 1986 attempted to block the fullblown policy of counterrevolutionary warfare. Meanwhile the administration tried to prevail on Costa Rica, El Salvador, Guatemala, and Honduras to coordinate military preparation in an alliance for a military showdown with the Sandinistas.

Latin American feeling runs high and when I was in the region, as I was on two trips to Mexico in 1984, I felt the Latin American expectation of an imminent U.S. invasion. The U.S. military action in 1983–1984 increased this expectation. Frederico Pagura's moderate voice as Methodist Bishop of Argentina and President of the Latin American Council of Churches is typical of what I have heard:

> The [U.S.] attack on the people of Nicaragua is an affront to all the people in Latin America and perhaps will definitively break our hope in the moral reserves of a people who were born invoking the protection of God and struggling for their own freedom.[6]

In Latin America in 1984, many talked of when (not if) the U.S. invasion would come. The cost of an invasion would be high because the majority of the U.S. people do not want to fight in Nicaragua to overthrow the Sandinistas. Even the report of the Kissinger Commission opposed military action by the United States unless a solid consensus could be formulated in favor of the action. The opposition by the U.S. public would be joined by the resentment of the majority in Latin America. Latin Americans do not have to love the Sandinistas to resent a U.S. invasion; their traditional hatred of U.S. military intervention in Latin America is reason enough. A friend of democracy, Jacobo Timerman, has addressed the resultant backlash of a successful overthrow of the Sandinista government:

> If the Sandinista government is toppled by the Reagan administration, its downfall will inevitably be converted into a symbol of the Latin American fight against the United States . . . if Reagan takes stringent action against Nicaragua, a banner of anti-Yangui solidarity will be hoisted over Latin America.
>
> That could have painful, perhaps savage results. U.S. embassies and companies would almost certainly come under attack.[7]

The last invasion of Nicaragua produced the three dictators of the Somoza family and a corrupt government. The record of the Sandinistas in human rights, education, health, and social justice is much better than that of the Somoza family, who were produced by a counterrevolutionary invasion by U.S. marines. As the leadership of the forces opposing the Sandinistas at this time is basically composed of former Somocistas, there is no reason to regard a victory by the Nicaragua Democratic Force (FDN) or by FDN in alliance with other Central American countries and the United States as capable of producing a better government than the Sandinistas'.[8]

Neither Christian theology nor the North American political traditions can deny that the oppressed Nicaraguans had just reason to rebel against the Somoza tyranny. The U.S. administration may dislike the Sandinista regime or its policies, but that dislike or repugnance gives no moral ground for making war on the new government. In fact, the United States is under solemn obligation in the treaty of the Organization of American States to refrain from intervention. Even the purchase of arms or the use of advisors from the Soviet Union or Cuba gives no moral ground for making war on Nicaragua. The question of the existence of arms trade between a country and a people in rebellion is not cause for war either. The Soviet Union gains no moral right to war on the United States because the United States supplies weapons, money, and goods to Afghan rebels. Nor does the United States gain a right to subvert Syria or India because they have received large shipments of arms from the Soviet Union. There are no moral grounds for attacking Nicaragua or for destroying the Sandinista government. Much morality consists of self-restraint, particularly regarding our weaker neighbors in Central America.

In El Salvador the landed oligarchy has ruled the country in a feudal manner and allied itself with Western financing and industrialism. The recent economic depression, inflation, and the destruction of the Central American common market have produced a situation of extreme economic deprivation. There is little evidence that the oligarchy or the army and politicians who serve it want to reduce their privileges or assist the peasants, workers, and unemployed. The domestic roots of the revolutionary movement go back to the early twentieth century and share some leadership with the Nicaragua movement.

The forces of the political center, including labor unions, universities, parts of the business community, the press, and progressive Roman Catholicism, have been repressed by the extreme right wing of the political spectrum allied with the army. The El

Salvador funds needed for development are shipped out of the country by the rulers, who demand more United States subsidies. Truly, in El Salvador the national-security state has taken over; it tolerates no dissent, the poor get poorer, and protestors get killed.

I have talked with refugees from El Salvador in *communidades de base* in Latin America and in sanctuary centers in the United States. They describe torture, rape, and murder run rampant under the leadership of the political right and the army. Thousands disappear and thousands more are killed in public by military and paramilitary forces trying fanatically to control the people. President Duarte at one time may have represented a democratic alternative to right-wing terror or popular revolution. But by now his government is characterized by terror, corruption, and disorder.

The United States Congress seems to be trying to slow down the vast amounts of U.S. dollars upon which Duarte, the oligarchy, and the army depend. The subsidy of El Salvador's government raises the question of whether this is the best use of U.S. funds during a time of government deficits and reduced funding to U.S. cities. The government is not worth supporting in any geopolitical calculation, the government is morally repugnant, and we become so by continuing to pay for it. Furthermore, the government is unable to defeat the insurgency. Whether the insurgents could defeat the government if it were denied U.S. help remains an open question. To me, it seems probable that without U.S. payment for counterinsurgency, the pressures for a negotiated solution granting sizable power to the forces now in revolt would prevail.

In any case, we cannot morally justify paying for the killing of those who resist the army and the oligarchy. So we must desist. If a killing is not justified it is murder, and that is an offense to reason and to God.

The North American churches have already established a consensus against the further imposition of U.S. will on El Salvador. The National Council of Churches, most large denominations, and the National Council of Catholic Bishops have all pleaded with the administration for a new direction. The statement of the Caribbean and North American Area Council of the World Alliance of Reformed Churches is typical: "The people of El Salvador should be allowed to solve their problems 'free from foreign intervention or interference,' a group representing 18 kindred denominations declared here today."[9] Several fundamentalist churches would disagree with the analysis of the majority of churches, since they would see the issue more as one of free people against Communists. However, an American administration already opposed by most denominations for subverting the Sandinistas and arming the government of El Salvador must certainly hesitate before undertaking a war in Central America.

The church's opposition to the war is demonstrated in its publications, educational programs, preaching, conferences, lobbying, letter campaigns, and so forth. The opposition is already reaching proportions reminiscent of the Vietnam War. There will be very little approval of American servicemen called to kill in Central America. What is more, the churches have already moved from petition and representative political opposition, which is a normal expression of Christian social concern, to patterns of resistance. These patterns of resistance represent a more extraordinary response to governmental policy. They say we will not cooperate with this killing. Though there are many forms of resistance, two are most noteworthy. One is the presence of North American Christians in likely invasion routes of Nicaragua. This Christian presence in villages near the border is a dramatic symbolic no to U.S. invasion. The second is the provision of assistance to refugees from Central America. This protection of refugees has been declared illegal by the Immigration and Naturalization Service (INS) though it would seem that the INS is itself in violation of the Refugee Act of 1980. The Supreme Court decision of March 9, 1987, against the Immigration and Naturalization Service, reinforced the claim that the clear intent of the 1980 law was to grant asylum as protection against persecution of refugees in their home countries. The trial of the church sanctuary leadership had only made the sanctuary movement a more visible form of protest against U.S. Central American policy.[10] Although I would not blame the United States as primarily responsible for the horror of El Salvador as some critics would, I see further involvement of a counterrevolutionary United States as a negative force that will only lead to innumerably more deaths, and at the end, even if the insurgents were all killed, the United States could not create a just government in El Salvador.

Struggle in the Churches

In 1973, I was involved in conversations in Jamaica with a vice-president of the Aluminum Company of America. We discussed the development of bauxite mines, the nationalization of bauxite in Guyana, and the politics of the new prime minister, Michael Manley. The vice-president expressed his opinion that politics in Jamaica could not become radical "because the people are so religious." It was fascinating to hear this connection between religion and political conservatism being asserted by a representative of a Pittsburgh-based transnational corporation.[11] The Rockefeller commission on Latin America conducted under Nixon's presidency noted that there were stirrings in the church and that if Catholicism in Latin America became radical it would shake the system. Of course, what has happened is that a portion of the churches in Latin America have connected their spirituality with their politics and made social revolution an option for Christian participation. Christianity, whether in Roman Catholicism, Protestantism, or Pentecostalism, is no longer a sure bulwark of the repressive status quo. In the move toward a social revolutionary Catholicism are heard memories of revolutionary priests in Mexican history and of the sixteenth-century Dominican *Bartolome de las Casas'* struggle to save the lives of the Caribbean and Central American Indians. Although it would be gross exaggeration to assert that Christianity in Latin America is now revolutionary, the struggle has been joined. Vital spirituality is now expressed in revolutionary directions as well as reactionary movements.

The most moving written expressions of the new action-oriented spirituality for me are found in Ernesto Cardenal's volumes of dialogue, *The Gospel in Solentiname.* These volumes are dialogues among peasants, priests, visitors, children, and adults around scriptural themes. They express two of the themes of the *communidades de base,* which are reforming some of Catholicism. These are lay interpretations of scripture and the application of scripture to the current social crisis. The community Cardenal founded at Solentiname was eventually destroyed by the Somoza national guard. This quiet, contemplative Trappist monk was finally pushed by social injustice and a repressive government to join the revolution.

He represents in a poignant way the movement from mysticism to social concern to social revolution. Now he participates in the Sandinista government as Minister of Culture. For a period he rejected the use of violence against the government, but gradually it became clear to him as it must to all who agonize over the enforcement of injustice that a season of violence was necessary to disarm the murdering national guard.

When Cardenal joined the revolution, close friends criticized him. Daniel Berrigan pleaded with him to renounce violence, arguing that no principle was worth the life of a child. Harvey Cox has described Cardenal's response to Berrigan:

> There was indeed no principle in the world that was worth the life of a child. He added, however, that the principle of pacifism had to be included, that the members of Solentiname—and with them many of the poor people of Nicaragua—had finally resorted to arms, and done so reluctantly, in order to defend children—and others—from murder. [12]

Christians cannot turn to armed resistance gladly. The use of violence is always that of a regretful moral necessity. It is sometimes Christian duty in an agonizing, sinful world to defend oneself and others against unjust violence. It seems to this teacher of Christian ethics that the case for the use of violence by Christians to prevent oppression and murder is clearly established. Cardenal has expressed well the classical position of Christian reluctant use of arms for the defense of children and others.

The use of pacifist-sounding principles by North Americans to criticize liberation theology is either founded in ignorance or preference for the national security systems of the oligarchies. North American Christians do not practice pacifism in their own national policies or frequently in their movements for social change. These citizens of perhaps the most violent power on earth have no moral standing to urge peasants and workers turned revolutionary to disarm before North American–equipped armies and terrorist squads.

Father Gustavo Gutiérrez participated in Pittsburgh Theological Seminary's 1976 celebration of the bicentenary of the American Revolution. He traced the origins of revolution in Latin American Catholicism and showed the tendencies of the North American liberal-revolutionary traditions to oppress the social-revolutionary movements of Latin America. He was repeatedly surprised by American-Christian criticism of liberation theology's recognition of the need to use violence to disarm the oppressors. For, from his Latin American vantage point, it was North Americans who had trained 50,000 to 70,000 Latin American army officers, provided the armaments for the national security systems, and in some cases paid for the support of the armies. In this respect liberation theology in the 1970s, like Christian realist theology in the 1930s, concludes that, given violent oppression, violent opposition to oppression is permitted.

Gutiérrez repeatedly stresses that Christians are not the originators of the revolution. Christians are allies with others in the revolutionary struggle. Neither Gutiérrez nor Cardenal would represent the Nicaraguan revolution as a Christian revolution. But it certainly is not an anti-Christian revolution. Many of the leaders in Nicaragua are Marxist, some are moderate democratic, and some are self-consciously Christian revolutionary.

Liberation theology, Gutiérrez repeats and repeats, is reflective thinking upon practice. Action precedes reflection. Christian theology reflects on revolutionary movements that have already begun. The goal of the reflection is to motivate Christians for the revolution, to clarify the processes of the revolution, to question ambiguous aspects of the revolution, and to struggle to maintain the humanitarian purposes of the revolution. Students of religion and society should be very clear that part of the praxis of liberation theology is revolution. When Gutiérrez was pushed to explain the purpose of his theology he finally expressed it briefly: "To seize power!" The commitment to social revolution is present in A Theology of Liberation.[13] Nicaragua in my judgment is the first of the liberation-theology social revolutions to accomplish two of the three forms of liberation. Liberation from the oppressor and liberation from fatalism and superstition. Of course, the group support, social organization, education, and communal action associated with liberation theology have accomplished a great deal in fostering human dignity throughout Latin America, but only in Nicaragua has the goal of seizing power been realized. Therefore the direction the revolution takes as it shapes Nicaragua will tell the world a lot about liberation theology's worth in practice. The uniqueness of Nicaragua has led Michael Novak and myself to regard Nicaragua as a suitable test case for liberation theology. Unfortunately, Novak has a strong ally in the Reagan administration, which also expects and wants the Nicaragua experiment to fail. The Reagan administration pressure may, of course, lead to the collapse of human rights and social development in Nicaragua. Certainly, it will move revolutionary Nicaragua toward the Soviet Union. The Soviet Union did not support the Sandinistas until after the success of the movement, and the small Communist party of Nicaragua opposed the Sandinistas, but U.S. violence drives them toward Soviet support. As Enrique Dussel, one of the best of the Latin American church historians said in Mexico City in 1984, "The enemy of my enemy is my friend." Consistent counterrevolutionary pressures and violence by the United States drives those whose natural sympathies are more with the United States toward the Soviet Union to find help from an "enemy of my enemy."

The Vatican, Protestant fundamentalists, and neoconservative Christians have all feared the association of liberation theology with Marxist analysis. Under the banner of anti-Communism, crude destruction of whole villages in Guatemala has been ruthlessly ordered by the rulers claiming Christ's sanction for murder. In Nicaragua, Christian expressions of anti-Communism are painted by the Contras on walls of villages they have ravaged. Christian anti-Communism rages on one side and a Christian-Marxist analysis informs many on the other side. Only the simplest rationalist could conclude that religion had no role in the struggle. Even though the Kissinger report on Central America does not study the religious issues, participants on both sides are dying with the name of Christ on their lips. The Central American style of absolute politics combines with the absolutism of religious movements to threaten religious crusades from the right and the left.

John Paul II is pressuring the priests not to go directly into revolutionary or political action. His scolding of Ernesto Cardenal was shown all over the world's press and on television during his 1983 visit to Nicaragua. Other Vatican statements criticize liberation theology's similarity in its social analysis to Marxism and its actual collaboration with Marxists. Some of John Paul II's concern comes from his own experience with the Marxism imposed on his native Poland. Despite the success of the church in maintaining itself in Poland, the struggle has been constant and has shaped the present pope. The evidence that Communist forces were involved in the attempt on his life cannot but encourage the pope to put distance between the church and Marxism. Even in Rome relations with Communist unions are not healthy, and conflicts between Marxists and Christians in Italian politics are normal. Why should a church that is more universal than Marxism cooperate with political parties in Central America that oppress it in Europe? To put the question in those terms implies a great deal of continuity between Central European parties and the Sandinistas. The implication is not completely justified. Even the communist party of Nicaragua is not the same as Communist parties in occupied Eastern Europe. There is more continuity within Catholicism than within communism, but even in Catholicism the national differences are striking. However, the history of antagonism between Catholicism and communism is too great for any rapprochement in the near future. I discussed the absence of liberation theologians in Rome with Father Bernard Haring in the spring of 1983. He said with a twinkle in his eye, "There are only six in the Curia and they are all my students." My conversations in the Vatican led me to understand that, although liberation theology may be read in the circles of power in Rome, it is not accepted to any large degree. There is some resistance to papal policy in Central America, but there is sympathy for the pope over the insults he received. The policy of the Vatican in Central America runs very close to a Polish heart, which still beats thanks to the failure of a Bulgarian-Communist plot. The Vatican will not restrain President Reagan from overthrowing the Sandinistas.

The differences between the Vatican's social theory and that of liberation theology are not absolute. The pope can refer to the differences between social classes, encyclicals can speak of imperialism by developed nations, the rights of private property are not absolute, the priority of the needs of the poor is recognized. The increasing richness in the Catholic church's discovery of social wisdom owes a great deal to Marxist analysis and challenge.[14] One does not expect the Vatican, however, to regard class analysis as the key to history, or to suggest that perhaps Marxism as a philosophy cannot be superseded, or that all of history revolves around an oppressor-oppressed axis, or to affirm revolution as a primary instrument of social change, or to rely as heavily on Marx's anthropology as Gutiérrez does in A *Theology of Liberation*.[15] The theologians of liberation cannot really expect the Vatican to accept their heavy dependence on several Marxian concepts. Marxism carries with it too much antireligious emphasis, and its history has been too filled with anti-Catholic repression for it to be accepted. Its reliance on historical materialism at the expense of more moderate sociological perspectives, its overemphasis on the positive results of revolution, and its unambiguous affirmation of humanity's creative powers all will prevent the liberation perspective on the utility of Marxism from being accepted in the center of Catholicism.

Liberation theology's use of Marxism reminds me of Christian realism's adaption of Marxist categories in the 1930s as seen in the journal called *Radical Religion* in this country or in the German *Neue Blatter*. In Germany and America, religious socialism flourished among intellectuals, and in America it allied with the labor union movement. It was crushed in 1933 by Hitler in its German version, and during World War II it faded in the United States. Gradually, Christian realism freed itself from any reliance on Marxism and based whatever surviving insights Marx had contributed on Christian theological principles. The great wisdom of Catholicism will best be served if liberation theologians are not repressed for their use of Marxist categories. History will sort out the validity of the Marxist ideas; those which are of God will survive and those which are futile will be forgotten. This is not said to stifle any critique of either Marxian or liberal-sociological ideas, but simply to suggest that critique, not repression, is what would dignify Christian discourse whether Catholic, Orthodox, or Protestant.

The hand of Gustavo Gutiérrez is evident in the documents of the conference of Latin American bishops from Medellin (1968) and Pueblo (1979). The priority of the church's ministry to the poor comes through both documents as does the denunciation of structured injustice. The documents of Pueblo as well as the pope's addresses made clear the announced commitment of the church to the poor. Poverty, which denied human rights and led to early death, is an offense to God. Poverty is seen as resulting from the sin of structured injustice. Pueblo hinted that the church itself is part of the problem.

> The luxury of a few becomes an insult to the wretched poverty of the vast masses. This is contrary to the plan of the Creator and to the honor that is due him. In this anxiety and sorrow the Church sees a situation of social sinfulness, all the more obvious because it exists *in countries that call themselves Catholic* and are capable of changing the situation: "[The exploited] have a right to have the barriers of exploitation removed, . . . against which the best efforts at advancement are dashed."[16]

As I have read liberation theology its analysis of poverty is fundamentally that the poor have been oppressed and are therefore poor. The invasions started in 1492, and Latin America has been exploited for the welfare of Europeans, indigenous elites, and North Americans since that time. The theory of dependency that liberal-international capitalism controls the markets, the finance, and therefore the structure of the world is a central link in the liberation understanding.[17] Liberation is in part the breaking of the chains of dependency, which tie poor people to the structure of international capitalism.

Liberation theology is an attempt to get Catholics in Catholic countries to be more practical and to join in the social revolution. The increasing identification of the church with the poor is seen as part of the process. The Pueblo phrase, which I underlined, points to another aspect of the problem. The problem of poverty in Catholic countries is partially Catholicism. No dominant religion can be shielded from a large degree of social responsibility for the cultural, economic, and political condition of the country it dominates.

It is widely recognized that the squalor of India is partially owing to the caste system and otherly-world focus of Hinduism. British colonialism is seen by many as responsible for the exploitation of India's wealth, and current economic structures of the international market do not favor India but it is Hinduism that has failed to encourage the human spirit to overcome poverty. Similarly, Catholicism, where dominant, has inspired too much passivity in the face of exploitation, too little economic dynamism, relatively nonproductive work habits, and less than economically helpful education.

Unfair structures whether international or domestic must either be overthrown or renegotiated. Revolution sometimes has a role to play in changing structures. Poverty however is overcome by the production and distribution of economic goods. The poor countries of Latin America do not produce enough product given their wildly growing populations to overcome the poverty of those populations. A revolution will not end poverty; at most, it will change the power relationships in society and give a new group a chance to effect economic change. The overcoming of a people's poverty requires their being organized to produce products or services that can be traded at prices that lift them out of poverty. Attitudinal and educational motivations are of primary importance. Can a social revolution in a Catholic population overcome poverty? Yes, but the restructuring of the public mind will need to produce attitudes radically different from those of the apathetic Catholicism that has existed in Latin America. But there are no guarantees of a revolutionary party overcoming poverty; witness Mexico with its experience of indigenous anti-Yankee revolution and continuing poverty. Economic planners and entrepreneurs may be more relevant to overcoming poverty than revolutionaries.

My own critique of liberation theology, which is more from a Weberian political-economic model than a Marxian model, finds faults with liberation theologians for (1) a neglect of the study of the responsibility of their Catholicism for the scandal of poverty, which Catholicism now raises its voice against, and (2) the paucity of economic analysis in their studies, which depend for their theological power on the critique of poverty.

A final area of concern in liberation theology is a problem for Roman Catholicism. The critique of Leonardo Boff's ecclesiology and his acceptance of the critique by the Vatican surfaces the issue.[18] Rome will not tolerate a people's church that supplants its own hierarchical patterns. The hierarchy of the church, the authority of bishops, and the claims of the pope will all be protected. The vision of many liberation theologians makes the church democratic and subject to the laity beyond what Rome will tolerate. The celebration of liberation theology as a second reformation foretells the struggle. Rome is in reformation as it slowly develops the implication of Vatican II; it will not allow its patterns to be overthrown by a peoples' movement within Catholicism. If the *communidade de base* movement grows, it may rupture relations between many Latin American Catholics and Rome. Whether in the long run such a rupture will encourage richer Christian life remains to be seen. In the short run it increases the vulnerability of Christians seeking social change. There is evidence that the *communidade de base* experience of solidarity in faith among the poor restores dignity to the poor. This could be the basis or beginning for the overcoming of poverty; my own limited experience from Mexico does not permit me to go beyond the recognition of having seen the poor receive their dignity. Dignity from the Latin *dignus* means a feeling of self-worth. It is necessary, as Allan Boesak reminds us, for mental health.[19] Dignity is discovered in the communal resistance to the oppressor. The courage to be against the oppressor receives a communal meaning and resists the forces of nonbeing. To give in to nonbeing leads to destruction and even to death itself. In the testimony of the people in communities overcoming the fear of the oppressors, which I have heard, violence is very clear as people find the courage of self-affirmation in community.

Obviously, socialist revolution is not on the foreseeable horizon of the major Latin American nations. The success of the Christian, moderate, Marxist alliance in the Sandinista coalition in Nicaragua in overcoming poverty needs to be evaluated. Nicaragua is very poor and the prospects of overcoming deprivation are not extremely high. If the coalition can achieve it, after U.S. pressure is reduced, it will contribute to optimism about liberation theology's future.

The basic practice of liberation theology is community organization around the ecclesiastical community for social change. This tactic is very powerful and remains valid even if the goal of socialist revolution is seen as inappropriate in many historical circumstances. The communities can function in their concrete situations without reference to socialist revolution. This certainly denies them, however, the fullblown promises of social liberation. It confines them to consciousness-raising reformist tactics. Meanwhile the pressures against the communities mount from the national security systems and the Vatican. The marginalizing of the communities threatens the movement for liberation. Dennis McCann's critique of liberation theology suggests the tension that characterizes the communities. It is unclear whether they will remain truly a mass-based movement, which will convert the church (Gutiérrez), or will become elite communities (Segundo), which may, by losing their spirituality, become only recruiting centers for secular liberation movements.[20] Even when the communities succeed as they did in Nicaragua, the question about the relevance of their commitments to actually overcoming poverty remains. The struggle against poverty is much more multifaceted than a commitment to socialist revolution. In fact, Hannah Arendt's classic study, *On Revolution*, concludes that though poverty is a motivation for social revolution, revolution is not effective in overcoming poverty. The historical records of both Marxism and dominant Catholicism are so miserable in overcoming poverty that the feasibility of the two in synthesis as an antipoverty force is doubtful.

However, skepticism about the economic future of Catholic-Marxism is not intended at all to support counterrevolutionary policies of the United States. The Somoza dictatorship in Nicaragua and the junta in El Salvador did not deserve to govern. United States support for Somoza and the oligarchy in El Salvador were both ill advised. The use of U.S. military force to overthrow the Sandinistas or to support Duarte, the army, and the oligarchy in El Salvador is immoral because it fails to meet the requirements of justified use of military force. A realistic approach to Christian peacemaking accepts both the necessity of revolution in Nicaragua and El Salvador and the rejection of and resistance to U.S. attempts at counterrevolution.

Alternative Models

The struggle between the Vatican and the liberation theologians is a Roman Catholic issue with profound consequences for Latin America. The second document inspired by Cardinal Joseph Ratzinger, "Instruction on Christian Freedom and Liberation,"[21] affirmed many of the themes of liberation theology while trying to separate Catholic social struggle from alliance with Marxism. The proscription of priests in political office, the preference for nonviolent political struggle, the warnings against groups that would impose foreign idcologies on cultures, and the criticism of revolution all separate the Vatican model of appropriate social action from that of liberation theology. Still the document allows dialogue to continue, and liberation theology seems to have won a place in the alternative strategies accepted by the Vatican. The document itself lacks a strategy for meeting the needs of the poor in Latin America. If it stripped liberation theology of its Marxist analysis and allies then liberation theology would also be bereft of strategy.

None of these models—Vatican, liberation theology, or Marxist—are very appealing to the Christian realist. None of the three have demonstrated a commitment to structuring procedures of producing and distributing wealth in a manner persuasive to the Christian realist. Christian realists who are caught up in pursuing the cold war perceive themselves as enemies of the experimentation among Marxist, liberation theologians, and others in Nicaragua. Christian realists committed to peacemaking wish Nicaragua's experiment well and they resist those in the United States who would crush the experiment. Christian realism does not expect North American intervention in Central America to produce social justice either. North American intervention in Central America violates international law and humanitarian principles as the World Court has ruled. The intervention's *means* are wrong. There are no defensible *ends* the United States intervention can serve because the instrument of intervention, the Contra force, is neither democratic nor humanitarian. Finally the intervention violates the virtue Christian realists have been urging on the United States: *self*-restraint. There are many things the United States with its power can do that it ought not to do. Violent intervention against a struggling social experiment in Nicaragua is one of those things from which the United States needs to restrain itself.

The model of social theology adopted by Gustavo Gutiérrez and others is indigenous to Latin America. Christian realism is indigenous to North America. Neither one is immediately relevant to the social issues of the other continent. Neither Gutiérrez nor Niebuhr understood the politics of the other continent very well. Niebuhr was innocent of Latin American experience; Gutiérrez has a little North American experience. Those who are persuaded of the relevance of Christian realism to the foreign policy of the United States will need to keep it from becoming an ally in the crushing of liberation theology in Central America.

Foreign policy powers are largely reserved to the administrative branch of government in the United States. Congress reserves rights constitutionally in the declaration of war, in ratification by the Senate of treaties, and in financing foreign policy. In difficult foreign policy questions, as in the questions of intervention in Central America, the administration has vast powers. But C.I.A. operations are subject to review, and finally Congress either finances or does not finance policy directions. In situations like the support of the Contras, shifting financial patterns on the part of Congress hinder the administration in the pursuit of its goals. However it is through congressional action that the moral and political will of the American people becomes imperfectly expressed. When the moral and political will of an administration is resisted by the American people through Congress the administration must either submit to that will or try to evade congressional actions.

The Henry Kissinger–chaired bilateral commission on Central America warned against attempting to use armed force in Central America without a united American consensus behind the action. The Reagan administration attempted to bypass congressional spending restrictions in financing the war against the Sandinista government. This led to secrecy, deception, and the enlistment of nongovernmental and other government funds coordinated by members of the National Security Council and the Central Intelligence Agency. As support for the Contras during a period of prohibition of U.S. funding for the Contras became revealed, the consequences to the administration were disastrous. The administration began to unravel as key personnel resigned or were dismissed. The ability of the administration to govern effectively was reduced, and the political influence of members of the administration diminished.

In 1987, it appeared that this clumsy process of regulating foreign policy through the funding process was taking hold and the engines of war vis-à-vis Nicaragua were being slowed. The forces of anti-Communism were not vanquished in open debate, but stalled because of the scandals surrounding the funding connections. The coalition government in Nicaragua seemed to be obtaining a chance to conduct their experiment.

The Arias peace plan, named for the president of Costa Rica, was in late 1987 providing opportunities for negotiations to end the armed struggles. Whether this attempt to turn from armed conflict to political struggle in Central America would succeed hung in the balance. Internal politics in Washington, D.C., remained a main variable in the process of turning toward regional solutions.

VII. DEVELOPMENT:
THE INDIAN EXAMPLE

Christian realism has influenced the intellectual life of the Indian Christian community and it can be seen in Kerala, the Christian Institute for the Study of Religion and Society, in theological seminaries, and in the writings of Christian intellectuals. M. M. Thomas has recently questioned the adequacy of Christian realism's perspective on questions of Indian development. Such questioning is needed; it points to the limits of Christian realism, which was developed primarily in North America. The founders of Christian realism, Reinhold Niebuhr and Hans Morgenthau, did not directly experience South Asia. Niebuhr had, of course, read Gandhi and attempted to meet him in London in 1931.[1] He regularly included examination of Indian religions in ethics classes and wrote about the struggle for democratic institutions in India. But his perspective was limited by the North American setting. A generation later, students influenced by Niebuhr had lived in India and were writing about India in a different light. Max Stackhouse of Andover-Newton Theological Seminary, Charles Ryerson of Princeton Theological Seminary, and Mark Jurgensmeyer of the Graduate Theological Union, Berkeley, are representatives of this group. So both in India and the United States there are significant groups of Christian intellectuals influenced by Niebuhr's thinking and writing about peacemaking and development in India. This generation most certainly agrees with Thomas that the cold war is not primarily a model for thinking about India. India is home to more people than live in both "superpowers." India's development will come out of a synthesis of the impact of technology and modern economics and the depth of India's religious culture. The experience and competition of the superpowers are neither irrelevant to India's development nor determinative.

The contrasts of India expose the visitor to sudden shifts in values, performance, and expectations. Disparate economic practices exist side by side, and Indian reactions to economic change or industrial tragedy are surprisingly different from North American responses. Nehru described the economic contrasts in his country: "Our country at the present moment is a very mixed country. Almost every century is represented in India: from the stone age in which some tribals live, you may say, to the middle of the twentieth century. We have atomic energy and we also use cow dung."[2]

Rajiv Gandhi's first budget only months after the industrial tragedy at Bhopal promised to open sectors of the Indian economy to transnational corporate entry. Rather than the greatest industrial accident resulting in tightening against transnationals, the new administration perception of economic realities led to relaxing restrictions against transnationals. The lowering of barriers to transnational corporations was accompanied by several tax concessions to the wealthy of India, an increasing national debt, and the reduction of regulations in the private sector enterprises. The reactions of Indian and American business communities were enthusiastic. The former rhetoric uniting development, growth, and social justice was displaced by a shift in emphasis to the private sector.[3] The former finance minister, V. P. Singh, talked in terms of "Gearing for take off," reflecting both old economic models of development and the prime minister's vocation as a pilot.[4] Neither Singh nor Gandhi, of course, expect transnationals to come into the country free of conditions, but the "welcome" mat has been extended. Early complaints contended that the lobbying efforts of the transnationals had directed the policy of the new government.

The industrial disaster of the Union Carbide plant in Bhopal dismayed the world. Casualty estimates vary from 1,500 to 5,000 dead because many of the dead were hurriedly buried in mass graves along with dead animals. The Delhi Science Forum estimated from on-site inspections in December of 1984 that the number requiring serious medical attention would be about 50,000.[5] The only parallel to the Bhopal suffering from gas would be the use of poisonous gas in wartime. In fact the phosgene, which was present in small amounts in the massive release of methyl isocyanate (MIC), has been used in gas warfare.

Questions have been raised about the outdated hazardous technology of the Bhopal plant. Its design and safety equipment were decidedly inferior to its West Virginia counterpart. The plant's staffing policies had been weakened since its installation, leaving an undertrained staff in charge of the hazardous technology. Perhaps the worst negligence in the plant involved the inoperative quality of many of the safety features of the plant. Crucial valves, the gas scrubber, and the flare tower were not in satisfactory condition. A ventilator line was being washed and the flare tower was scheduled for repairs at the time of the accident. Motors needed for pumping gas to the scrubber were shut down and the central panel monitors were operating unsatisfactorily. The chilling unit, which is necessary to control any runaway reactions in MIC, had been off for a period of time as an economy measure. In short, the plant was in hazardous condition at the time of the accident.

The scientific reports released in India substantiate a picture of bad management and negligence. In addition to safety functions being inoperable, and negligence on the part of workers, the information furnished by Union Carbide to the government of Bhopal or to the local people was inadequate. The medical response was clumsy owing, again partially, to Union Carbide's noncooperation in sharing information. Government relief work was slow and confused. Negotiations for compensation between Union Carbide and India broke down. The development of criminal charges unfortunately has not progressed. The plant was closed and workers let go, but the implications of the accident for future importation of hazardous technology are in doubt. In court, Union Carbide countered the foregoing interpretation by charges of industrial sabotage by disgruntled employees. However, on July 24, 1987, Union Carbide agreed to pay penalties of $408,500 to settle Occupational Safety and Health Administration charges of hundreds of willful safety violations in the United States. The Union Carbide plant in West Virginia had released toxic gas in 1985 sending 100 persons to the hospital. After much delay and years of defense in the courts, Union Carbide has offered to provide half a billion dollars as settlement to India for the Bhopal catastrophe. The issue remained in the Indian courts in early 1988.

The violence of industry in India is overshadowed by the daily reports of intercommunal violence in some parts of India. Personal violence seems comparable to that of North America, but the continuing communal conflicts dominate the news.

The religious violence against Mrs. Gandhi, which elevated Rajiv

Gandhi to power, has its economic roots in the disputes over the agricultural wealth of the Punjab as the caste riots in Gajurat are over reservations in education, which provide quotas for "backward classes." Deprivation and the struggle over resources directly relates to the violence of the Indian subcontinent. Dialectically, the caste system, which is struggled over in Gujarat, is implicated in the poverty that provoked the struggle. The wealth of the Sikhs, which they try to protect, is in Punjab's "Green Revolution" agriculture, which depends on intensive use of pesticides like that produced in Bhopal. The struggle for advantages in education is in part a struggle for technological qualifications, which will lead out of poverty. Technology, education, agriculture, and industry are all tied in together in the system that produces so much violence.

Can development reduce the violence in India? What are the prospects for development and how does American transnational corporate power relate to India? Do the churches have a significant role in advising on transnational corporate policy? The first draft of the U.S. bishops' pastoral letter on Catholic social teaching and the U.S. economy, stresses the interdependence of the world and the importance of the decisions of transnational corporations in shaping that world. It quotes John Paul II: "Yes, development is the new name for peace. Peace is necessary. It is an imperative of our time. And so is this development or progress; the progress of all the disadvantaged."[6] Peace means development in Catholic social teaching and particularly it means a "preferential option for the poor." The Presbyterian Church's "Toward a Just, Caring and Dynamic Political Economy" sees a "special concern for the poor and oppressed" as a requirement of God's justice. Policies and systems are to be evaluated by what they do for all and particularly for the poorest. In Luke 4:18-19, the proclamation of Good News for the poor by Jesus is taken as the continuation of the prophetic message of justice. In Matthew 25:31-46, *nations* are judged by Jesus by what they have done for the least who were hungry, in prison, or thirsty.[7] *Shalom* in its broad meanings includes justice, which makes for welfare. So peace includes development of the poorest, and the prospects for this development is the inquiry of India today.

The World Council of Churches (W.C.C.), whose existence corresponds to the modern post–World War II rise of the transnational corporation, has wrestled with issues of economic justice throughout its life. Eschewing both laissez-faire capitalism and communism, the

W.C.C. has held up a model of the responsible society. Gradually it has come to reject the order being developed by the transnational corporation (TNC). The W.C.C. has spoken of its norms as a vision, which is useful for evaluating TNCs and as a guideline for formulating strategies. The three norms, middle axioms, or guidelines are justice, participation, and sustainability.[8] Practice in India and most of the rest of the world violates the norms. The caste system denies both equality and freedom, which are the constitutive parts of justice. Most of the society does not participate in the modern economy; in fact, to the degree that participation requires literacy, most of the people are denied participation since only 36 percent are literate. Sustainability is very much in question as the combination of poor agricultural policies, deforestation, and the threats of the Green Revolution combine, and exploding population threatens to collapse the ecosystem. The distribution of wealth in India has no relationship to justice, and the gap between the starving poor and the overconsuming rich is growing. While 50 percent of the population is below the poverty line at $300 in U.S. annual income, 136,000 Indian tourists spent $42.5 million in England alone in 1983.

The Indian middle class has been increasing in visibility and power. In an article celebrating the rising middle class, *India Today* editorialized: "For all that, however, there is no getting away from the fact that even if *the poor will always be with us*, so will the middle class from now on."[9]

The use of the quote from Jesus in Matthew 26:11 in a popular English journal in India points to the popularity of the text and its use regularly as an excuse to accept poverty. In the quoted text the reality of poverty seems just to be acknowledged as "fact" and the emergence of a middle class celebrated. Sometimes that text is used in a crude way to justify the conditions that keep people poor.

Larry Rasmussen and Bruce Birch have argued that the misuse of the text points to the need to examine the entire canon before giving a text on an ethical issue biblical authority. Any cruel interpretation of the text violates Jesus' concern for and ministry to the poor throughout his ministry according to the gospel records. The content of the text makes clear that he was defending the generous act of a woman from overly stringent criticism from his followers. Any stingy interpretation of the text flies in the face of the overwhelming biblical commitment to concern and legislation to protect the poor. The quoted text itself is so similar to a text in Deuteronomy that it suggests "the possibility that

Jesus is directly referring to it."[10] This discussion of poverty in Deuteronomy seems to stand behind the quote in Matthew, Mark, and John attributed to Jesus. In its immediate context in Deuteronomy, it seems to be part of the discussion of lending money to fellow Hebrews. In Jesus' use it is the defense of a generous act. In the Indian-American situation it is important that the suggested images of the quote not be used to deaden protest against poverty. As the middle-class priorities are expressed in the new Indian budget, the consequences for the poor are feared.

The Bible is realistic about poverty. There is no need for poverty. The world God has created is rich enough for all, but in our sin we have defied God and the world, producing poverty. Since we have the poor with us, we must meet their needs. Deuteronomy 15 expresses this biblical realism about poverty beautifully. The text of the chapter is a whole series of regulations for protecting the poor in Israel. The text says: "There will be no poor among you (for the Lord will bless you in the land which the Lord your God gives you for an inheritance to possess), if only you will obey the voice of the Lord your God, being careful to do all this commandment which I command you this day" (Deuteronomy 15:4-5). But immediately after the promise of no poverty if the commandments are fulfilled is the legislation for caring for the poor: "You shall not harden your heart or shut your hand against your poor brother, but you shall open your hand to him, and lend him sufficient for his need, whatever it may be" (Deuteronomy 15:7c-8). Realism demanded the recognition that the poor were present, that the commandment had not been kept. So recognizing the presence of this poverty from sin, the Deuteronomic author admits and urges: "For the poor will never cease out of the land; therefore I command you, You shall open wide your hand to your brother, to the needy and to the poor, in the land" (Deuteronomy 15:11).

There is little justice in India and yet only in justice can peace be found. The Bible is clear: "And the effect of righteousness will be peace, and the result of righteousness, quietness and trust for ever. My people will abide in a peaceful habitation, in secure dwellings, and in quiet resting places" (Isaiah 32:17-18). The impact of American, British, and other transnationals on an unjust India can only compound the injustice, for the lack of justice in America and Great Britain is transmitted through the economic-social policies of the transnational corporation into the injustice of India.

The bishops' pastoral on economy grounded its norms in reflection on the biblical themes of:

(1) Creation, Covenant, and Community
(2) The Primacy of Justice
(3) Wealth and Poverty
(4) Discipleship and Social Justice

The development of these biblical and theological themes into ethical norms and an examination of the economic system of the world led them to a severe critique of U.S. international developmental policy and to a call for reform in the international economic order. The ethical norms developed included:

(1) Human Rights
(2) Justice and Participation
(3) Justice as Requiring Institutional Priorities
(4) Diverse Economic Agents as Having Particular Responsibilities and Rights

Wherever on Protestant, Roman Catholic, or ecumenical ground the church approaches the economic order from a normative standpoint, it takes a critical stand vis-à-vis the major international economic actors. The pope put it most plainly at Edmonton in 1984:

> In the light of Christ's words (Mt. 25:35-36) this poor South will judge the rich North. And the poor people and poor nations—poor in different ways, not only lacking food, but also deprived of freedom and other rights—will judge those people who take these goods away from them, amassing for themselves the imperialistic monopoly of economic and political supremacy at the expense of others.[11]

Whereas both the bishops' pastoral and the W.C.C. policies can be read as rooted in a systemic rejection of the transnational corporate policies, Protestant churches in the United States have not developed policy vis-à-vis transnational corporations.

A major study of the churches and transnational corporations by the Presbyterian Church tended to affirm the role of transnational corporations. The study "The Church and Transnational Corporations"[12] indicated that although there was no church policy on the corporations, church members were told that work within the corporations served God's intent for human welfare.[13] Though Richard Barnet served for a while on the committee preparing the report, the sharp critique of transnational corporations found in the book he coauthored with Ronald E. Muller, *Global Reach*,[14] was infrequently found in the study book.

Forces Resisting Development

Development as used in theological literature means the organization of society so that human beings can flourish as children of God. It has an economic dimension and where the produce of people is insufficient for their welfare it means the growth of their production. When the produce of a people is too great for their welfare, development means reducing their production or radically sharing their production. It means the reform of political and social institutions so that humanizing growth is not choked by bureaucracy or tyranny. It implies a forward movement toward a more just society in which the powers of each human being are expressed and not repressed. The concept of development expresses the three-dimensional means of Gustavo Gutiérrez's concept of liberation: liberation from the oppressor, liberation from forces of fate, and liberation to community with God and neighbor.

So the concept of development is eschatological, it is the vision of human fulfillment, and it is immediately practical, giving us our task for today. One of my favorite visions of development is from Isaiah. It tells me what development means; it implies a transformation of India:

> No more shall there be in it an infant that lives but a few days, or an old man who does not fill out his days. . . . They shall build houses and inhabit them; they shall plant vineyards and eat their fruit. They shall not build and another inhabit; they shall not plant and another eat; for like the days of a tree shall the days of my people be, and my chosen shall long enjoy the work of their hands. They shall not labor in vain, or bear children for calamity; for they shall be the offspring of the blessed of the Lord, and their children with them . . . . They shall not hurt or destroy in all my holy mountain, says the Lord.
> (Isaiah 65:20-25)

Authors in both India (for example, S. Swaminathan[15]) and in the West (for example, Charles Elliott[16]) are agreeing that development must be humanistic. Women, including Devaki Jain, have reminded us that development cannot be humanistic until the perspectives and resources of women are involved in determining the paradigms for development.[17] Devaki Jain has shown how the search for development must proceed through the use of ambiguous resources. As a feminist she can find in Gandhi, who must remain ambiguous as an advocate of women, resources for autonomy, self-sufficiency, self-realization, and social transformation needed for a woman's paradigm of development. Despite the ambiguity of Hinduism on women, she finds resources of individual autonomy and goals of self-realization, which she regards as necessary for development.[18]

Gunar Myrdal's classic work on development in South Asia, entitled *The Asian Drama*, is subtitled *An Inquiry into the Poverty of Nations*. Since the book is largely focused on India, it provides an encompassing survey of the reasons for the resistance to development in India.

(1) Despite the difficulty of ascertaining exactly the inhibiting features of climate upon development, they must be recognized. Because capital is scarce the climatic conditions are hard to counter. Myrdal thinks that the "extremes of heat and humidity" contribute to wearing down the soil, material goods, and people. The low productivity of some crops, animals, and forests is also related to climate. The aridness of much of India also contributes to the trend toward desertification following deforestation. The tropical climate not only causes discomfort, it reduces health and efficiency.[19]

(2) The population growth in India has preceded its industrial economic development. The poor seek economic security by having children. Every gain in production is rapidly consumed by a growing population, and underemployment, which drags the whole society down, is almost a necessity because of the population. Schools and health facilities fail to keep up with the population growth and the press of population embitters the struggle for survival. Gains in health and literacy have been made by the masses since independence. These gains have been slow, and responses from abroad have been inadequate to the magnitude of the task.

(3) India has only 1 percent of the international trade of the world. Trading relationships have been imposed by the more powerful Western corporations. The early experience with a transnational corporation led to India's being governed by the East India Company and its wealth taken by the British. It is reported that Great Britain took out of India up to 10 percent of India's G.N.P. in the last years of the

nineteenth century. Even today many of the transnational corporations' sales are greater than India's national budget. The development
of the power of the TNCs imposes great disadvantages on a nation
trying to achieve just economic relationships. Previous European
periods of growth were based on the ability to export products, so the
possibility that India can become a significant exporting nation is
slim.

(4) Social inequality and fatalism about one's role in the world are
rooted in the culture and religion of India. This religiously sanctioned
inequality and fatalism are institutionalized in the desperate poverty of
more than 300 million people. Resources are not available for
investment on the part of these millions; every resource is needed for a
meager subsistence. The religious sanction of squalor is doubly
difficult because you cannot normally develop a people while
opposing their religion, yet much of their religious tradition sees no
need for development. Since they lack development and opportunity,
corruption increases and makes development even more unlikely.
The social planners predict development, but like predictions of the
disappearance of Hinduism or the elimination of caste, it is not
evident. The new prime minister got into difficulty by saying that
Calcutta, the nation's largest city, was dying. Newspaper editorials
and columnists discussed the remark for weeks; Bengalis argued that
there was a lot of life in a dying Calcutta. It was a mixed picture. No
one predicted a renaissance for Calcutta. The response from the less
defensive, non-Bengali section of the country was, "Aren't all of our
cities, except Delhi dying?" Decline is in the air. Although the
pessimism is expressed most openly by educated Moslems and
English-speaking southerners, it can be seen architecturally all across
the country. The country is not being maintained.

Among Christians in India, M. M. Thomas has identified the
social roots of underdevelopment as clearly as anyone: "No economic
measures can succeed in India unless simultaneously there is a
struggle against the social and cultural framework within which the
traditional economic mechanism functions."[20]

(5) Technology is commanded by institutions most interested in
transferring profits to home institutions. Technology developed in its
modern period in a Europe that had experienced a Renaissance, a
Reformation, and an Enlightenment. Europe, North America, and
Japan have integrated the technology into their systems in a manner
that gives their transportation, financial, production, and advertising

facilities overwhelming advantages in competing with domestic entrepreneurs in India. The TNCs are efficient at draining capital out of a country. They are only peripherally interested in the humanistic development of a potential market. The TNCs have powers to reward richly or to punish severely national groups whose support or fear they need. The British policy could basically be seen as keeping India a poor agricultural hinterland for Great Britain. The larger portion of outside investment in India is still British, and I see no reason to conclude that corporate goals are more benign now than under Victoria. Nor is one moved to expect more generosity from Japanese or American transnationals. An area in which technology has produced a valuable essential to economic development is in agriculture. Economic underdevelopment in India has been owing partially to its low agricultural output. The Green Revolution has increased that output. Even though the Green Revolution was unaccompanied by the social reform necessary to make its benefits widely dispersed and to minimize its social dislocation, it has increased the food supply, the trade balance, and the G.N.P. The cost of displaced agricultural workers, middle-income farmers displacing poor farmers, increased agribusiness, and the heavy use of chemical fertilizers and pesticides are still to be reckoned.

Indian poverty is the result of a particular cumulative history. Cultural and religious attitudes combine with an exploding population, in a nonrich land dominated by transnational corporate forces and national forces uninterested in social justice, which leaves a people suffering grotesquely under poverty and injustice. it is a country without peace.

Action for Development

The action potential for development is very broad, ranging from influencing international structures to changing individual attitudes. As the causes of poverty are cumulative, so too the impetus for development is multicausal.

Prime Minister Rejiv Gandhi's first Finance Minister, V. P. Singh, presented India's requests for changes in international finance to the interim committee of the International Monetary Fund in April 1985. He urged harmonization of industrial-power policies so that interest rates could be lowered and exchange rates stabilized. He urged industrial countries to reduce policies of protectionism so that developing countries could export more easily. He called for increased development-assistance aid to offset the deterioration in the amount of aid available. He asked for Special Drawing Rights on the IMF for developing countries, and for a truly international conference to revise the financial arrangements of the international system. The Indian initiative reflected agenda items of the New World Economic Order Plan, and the negative response of leading financial powers left little prospect for substantial movement in the directions posed by V. P. Singh. The proposals represent a substantial consensus among the developing nations of structural changes they require to stimulate economic growth. Structural changes like those envisaged by V. P. Singh have been widely supported by Christian groups studying development. The need is obvious for the United States to play a positive role in empowering the powerless through revising international structures. The official U.S. response however is negative, and emphasis is put on the beneficial aspects to the world of U.S. growth and the benefits of direct investment by U.S. corporations rather than an increase in aid. As the Indian theologian Osthathios put it: "voluntary poverty is a joy and structural poverty a burden. But as a voluntary poverty cannot be expected from the worldly rich, ways must be found out by those who are ready to suffer to empower the powerless to make the powerful share their power with the powerless."[21]

But voluntary adjustments are not now in the immediate future. India's own plans must be developed.

The Seventh Five-Year Plan for India calls for greater consumption by its middle class. The budget for 1985–1986, referred to earlier, announced greater rewards for the private sector and a diminished role for the public sector in the Indian mixed economy. India theoretically has the instruments for planning for which many reformers and proponents of industrial policy in the United States would hope. However, India is not good at collecting taxes, executing plans, or controlling corruption. The nation is torn by feudal social practices, communal and sectarian strife, and caste conflict.

Immediate pressing issues for development require getting ten million children out of the exploitative labor market and into education, which will equip them for a dynamic rather than a servile role in the Indian economy.

A water plan must be enacted that would enable the irrigation necessary for the projected doubling of agricultural production needed by the year 2000. Drinking water is as much a crisis issue as is the need for irrigation. The needs are real, and employment in meeting desperate infrastructure needs, as in water, would benefit development.

A 36 percent literacy rate stifles development, and immense programs of adult and child literacy education must precede development.

Basic health concerns remind one of Gandhi's campaign to save the Harijans from their roles as cleaners and carriers of human excrement. The campaign still needs to be waged. The shift in attitude toward the removal of human waste would create another industry, and it points to the reality of employment in sewer construction.

Development requires stringent requirements to keep Indian trained medical personnel in the country. India can afford to export some of its workers and to benefit from the return of their salaries to the country, but health care in India is very undernourished; the physicians, health workers, and nurses are needed in India.

After the international agencies and the national government, the TNC contribution to development may be the most significant. These actors provide some technological transfer, some investment capital, and some expertise. The commitment to worldwide profit maximization, however, limits the positive contribution of the TNCs. Indian critiques of the TNCs stress that the Indian population is not allowed to participate meaningfully in the decisions of the TNC actors. The technology transferred is often inappropriate to the Indian needs and it is seldom the most advanced. It comes with restrictions that limit Indian exploitation of the technology. The patent expenses for the use of Western technology drain off resources for development; although there are gains from TNC presence in the country, it tends to corrupt the Indian political process as the Indian elite is coopted by Western interests. The advertising of the TNCs encourages overconsumption by the rich and a preference for foreign goods over domestic products. Nonessential needs are encouraged to grow and the necessities of the poor are made more difficult to meet by the TNC trading patterns.

Of course, the TNCs will be involved, because they dominate the world economic system, but part of the struggle for development will be the criticism from India of their practices. The goal of profit maximization inevitably conflicts with the needs of the poor in India.[22] The U.N. has responded to criticism of the TNCs by study and recommendations, which present a comprehensive plan for channeling the usefulness of the TNCs into development while regulating their power. Of course, international agencies are still too weak to regulate TNCs, which are bigger in economic clout than most governments. Regional agreements among developing countries on joint understandings for TNCs may be more effective. The control of developing economics by TNCs can be somewhat mitigated by host countries insisting on joint ventures, consortium approaches, and coproduction agreements. [23]

Finally, of course, the Western countries are going to have to assert their own sovreignty and correct biases in tax laws that favor TNCs moving production abroad, regulate companies which use the social product of the country's technology, democratize the boards that control the industries, force corporations to honor the welfare of the communities, which have contributed to the corporations, demand public accounting by the corporations, and the release to the public and the state of accurate information on company policies. The TNCs are too big for the United Nations; their own home countries will have to control them and encourage countervailing power in labor, state, and local government, and voluntary organizations.

Voluntary organizations maintain the varieties of social experimentation, which is necessary if a significant degree of development is to take place. These groups can encourage alternative life-styles freed from conspicuous consumption. They provide the training and the start-up funds for dozens of small centers of production. Much of the health, welfare, and educational work in India is carried on by voluntary associations. The churches have been particularly crucial in developing the medical resources and educational foundations of India. The restrictions on missionaries will mean, however, that more of the educational mission of the church will have to be carried on by Indians themselves. Whether India's ethos will support relevant education to the degree necessary to prepare leaders to help the people remains to be seen.

Charles Elliott's research into development found the church's most relevant work: (1) in shared development where, on the Ecumenical Development Corporation model, funds and power of decision were jointly developed by donor and the local development personnel; (2) in the conscientization of marginal peoples of the society for social development. In India, Catholic priests influenced by liberation theology have been actively helping fishers to organize in Goa and Kerala to defend their economic interests, and they have had some success. Generally speaking the church exists in India among marginal sectors of the population, and its future contribution to society depends to a degree on its own empowerment and improved education.[24]

The work of voluntary organizations in poor countries and in rich countries in the boycott of Nestle products to develop company policy in a more humane way is a precedent for the strategies of voluntary organizations countering cruel TNC policies. Development strategies of churches, voluntary organizations, and governmental bodies designed to counter corporate policies allied to racism or militarism reflect part of the multifaceted approach to development. Development in the sense used in theological literature is thwarted by both racism and militarism and part of the development struggle for peace is to reduce those evils.

Many of the most successful development projects have come out of women's organizations. The women of India are among the poorest of the poor, but they are showing a resilience and a fighting spirit that promises development from the grass roots. Women's movements have been able to use Gandhian strategies of decentralization, home-based production, subsistence economy rather than exchange economy, control of the means of production, the development of human consciousness, and the maximization of local traditions to create new models for Indian development.[25] Women's control over their own bodies is part of the struggle for development. The population problem is necessarily part of the overall development strategy, but it cannot be meaningfully shaped by either international corporate interests or the Roman Curia's teaching. The corporate interests dump unsafe birth control practices on poor women, and Rome will not accept rational human control over reproduction. Until men can be conditioned to care, the main burden of control of reproduction in India will fall on the women and their organizations. The women's models for development are not complete, their emergence calls for more research, particularly into how far women can use their traditional religious heritage for development.

Development in India requires not only more will than is evident, but more research. Myrdal's massive research pointed again and again to how little is known about the causes of underdevelopment and how much more must be learned about development. International organizations, transnational corporations, national governments, and voluntary associations all need to multiply the inquiries into the process of overcoming the poverty of India.

This chapter, of course, does not exhaust the subject of development. It is only an introduction to the subject by one who is a novice to India. Others will perhaps be stimulated by its omissions and errors to carry the work farther. The conclusion is simple: Peace in India requires development. Peacemaking is the struggle against great odds for that social transformation called in our time development. [26] A few miles from where I lived in Bangalore, the words "The work of Government is God's work" are inscribed over the state capitol building. If the work of the government is the rigorous pursuit of human development, the words are true. If not, the words are dangerous, for they claim ultimacy for politics without purpose. From Psalm 103 came the word of the Lord to me in the terrible poverty of India:

> The Lord works vindication and justice for all who are oppressed.
>   (Psalm 103:6)

Overcoming poverty in India requires immense shifts in human consciousness. The human dedication to investment in military expenditures dwarfing educational and health expenditures has to be overcome. Listening to the poor and accepting their priorities for food, fuel, water, and education over profit and bureaucratic necessity will need to become a priority. The fitting of technological development to human needs rather than to the West's needs for transfer of funds is required. The development of the positive resources in traditional religions to overcome fatalism is essential. So the task of realistic peacemaking through development for India fits Max Weber's aphorism for a moral politics: "It is the slow boring of hard boards."

VIII. RESPONSE TO RELIGIOUS ROOTS OF TERRORISM

The foreign policies of the administrations of both Presidents Carter and Reagan came unraveled in Iran. Neither group of policy makers could find a way to deal with terrorism and the taking of hostages. The debacle of the aborted rescue mission, the humiliation of the hostages in the Tehran embassy, and the releasing of frozen bank accounts weakened the presidency of Jimmy Carter. President Reagan's image of a strong presidency was seen to be hollow as close advisors carried out ransom shipments from the U.S. arsenal to Iran to free the hostages. The knowledge that Iran had also encouraged and probably funded blowing up the U.S. embassy and Marine barracks in Beirut revealed an administration in over its head in Middle Eastern foreign policy. One part of the administration was seen as haranguing U.S. allies not to resupply Iran while another part was delivering weapons to Iran for its war with Iraq, which the United States was also aiding.

In Iran the Reagan administration came up against reality. It was a reality foreign to the dreams of the administration. Robert McFarlane did not have the clout to realize the president's dreams for "moderates" in Iran. Khomeini took the weapons, paid for them, his followers released a few hostages, and then took more hostages. The president painted dreamlike pictures of never ransoming hostages while doing just that. One critic of the failures of Reagan policy described the Reagan administration as awash in sentimental neoconservative idealism. The beginning of recovery would be a return to realism.

If American foreign policy is to recover from the moral and intellectual intoxications of the Reagan years, it must be recalled to realism, to the

138

theoretical and practical advantages of seeing the world as it is, of measuring action not by its inspirations but by its consequences, of cleaving as closely to the facts and interests as to values.[1]

Realism requires a recognition of the limits of arms diplomacy and the existence of a powerful religious-political movement spreading from Tehran through Lebanon. It requires a recognition of the futility of the Contra operation and the staying power of Sandinista influence in Nicaragua. It does not serve the nation's honor or interest to bargain for hostages and deny it, or to mine Nicaraguan harbors while supporting a force composed of Somocistas and calling them the "moral equivalent of our founding fathers."

A realistic approach to foreign policy does not entail secretly bargaining away the U.S. arsenal to recover hostages. It may require punishment of those who take Americans hostage. The punishment will need to be administered with the traditional moral understandings governing the use of violence. Above all it requires the keeping of the main directions of U.S. foreign policy clear. Policy once articulated cannot be overthrown out of sentiment for hostages.

Terrorism is difficult to define. The word retains a pejorative meaning. As is often said, one country's terrorist is another country's freedom fighter. But despite the difficulty, an attempt at definition is required for understanding. It is understood that the defining process requires a stipulation that reflects the perspective of the one undertaking the definition.

One begins to inquire about terrorism, knowing that a lot more is said about the subject than is known. The *International Encyclopedia of the Social Sciences* does not have an entry on terrorism; undoubtedly the next edition will have a lengthy essay. On the other hand, the Bible contains a lot of references to terror. A theologian may permit himself or herself here a humble reference to the relevance of the scripture.

However the use of terror in the scripture does not define our subject. For here it does not come from the poor of the earth or from totalitarian states, but from God in protecting Jacob (Genesis 35:5) and in assisting Israel in conquering the promised land (Exodus 23:27). In Job, Leviathan is the source of terror (ch. 41). Isaiah speaks of the terror of the Lord (2:10, 19, 21). In Romans, the government is a terror to evil conduct. In Luke, Jesus foresees terror from the skies (21:11).

Terrorism, as defined for our reflection, will not contain all of these scriptural understandings. However, following the example of the Bible it ought not to be too narrowly defined. The definition will not restrict terrorism to either Leviathan or God, but neither will it exclude governments from terrorism. A definition should not necessarily cast moral guilt on its source. It is helpful to remain open to the possibility, at least at the definitional stage, that its source may be a legitimate government, or even, as many terrorists believe, God.

Because of the extreme debates about the morality surrounding the term *terrorism* it is most useful to try to stipulate a morally neutral definition, though the term itself makes this difficult. A modification of Harold Lasswell's definition would read, Terrorism is participation in the political process, which strives for political results by arousing acute anxieties through the use of violence.[2]

This general definition of terrorism is open to the meaning of terror in Paul's understanding of government and reminds us of the association of terror with revolutionary governments' purges, as in "the terror" of the French Revolution. Governments deliver to terror those whose behavior they find offensive. A few Western democracies and their heirs to parliamentary government around the world try to cooperate with opposition and permit an alteration between opposition and ruling parties. But in most countries opposition is subject to terror.

Terrorism has the same root meaning as *deterrence*; both come from the Latin word *terrere*, to make afraid. Nuclear terror, the arousing of acute anxieties, has been an act of U.S. policy to achieve political goals in several situations.[3]

The third modern use of terrorism is that of state terror against international opponents. In the Middle East it is documentable that numerous states use both terror and assassination to promote their international aims. Libya, Iran, Iraq, Syria, and Israel have been prominent players in the use of terror to advance their aims. *The New York Times* reports of an alliance of twenty-two Libyan, Syrian, Palestinian, Lebanese, and other groups to combat U.S. policy in the Middle East. The United States' support of the Contra forces is another example of the use of terrorist policy to achieve national goals on the international scene.

There is also a network of nongovernmental groups using terror to achieve political purposes. These range from groups representing Palestinians to both sides of the Northern Ireland conflict, to Moslems in the Philippines, the Red Army in Italy, Sikh militants in India, and Tamil organizations in Sri Lanka. Some groups cooperate with other groups. Funding and organizational patterns shift with changing political tides. Some of these groups, particularly the Provisional IRA and Sikh groups, receive sanctuary, and sometimes training and funding, within the United States.

Though often taken less seriously than the groups just discussed, patterns of terrorism are associated in the United States with the Ku Klux Klan, Posse Comitatus, and other paramilitary organizations.[4]

So, we can see that the United States is deeply implicated in terrorism. In fact, in my own neighborhood a cross was burned four years ago to terrorize a black family. Commentators argue that the United States can accomplish little until it abandons its own open support of terrorism.[5] Support for the Contra forces particularly is seen by non-American observers as support for terrorism. India regards both North America and Canada as soft on Sikh terrorists. The British rightfully see the U.S. protection of Provisional Irish Republican Army refugees as supporting terrorism.

However, extirpating the terrorism from domestic politics and the international policies of the United States seems beyond our capacities. We may, however, take some steps to reduce its cost to us and to reduce its frequency.

An analysis of any of the groups just mentioned would require a longer chapter than is intended here. However, the depth of the religious, political, economic, and cultural causes of terrorism must be considered before we can speak of a Christian ethical response to any of the movements. The religious roots of the terrorism from Iran need to be comprehended before a sensible response can be developed.

The Shiite Crusade

One of the more important political ideologies of the twentieth century is the religion-inspired Shiite crusade to rid the Middle East of American dominance. There are 832 million Moslems in seventy nations composing almost one fifth of humanity. The crusade is led by the followers of Shia Islam under the direction of the Ayatollah Khomeini. Shia, the part of Islam most inclined to violence, comprises 10 percent of the followers of Islam. The Shiite crusade is also joined by many Sunni militants.

The Shiite revolution has taken power only in Iran, where Shiites compose about 88 percent of the population. Shia is also the majority religion in Iraq and the island nation of Bahrain. Lebanon has about 30 percent of the population identified as Shiites. Pakistan contains about 12 million Shiites, India approximately 10 million, and the Soviet Union 4 million.[6] The success of Khomeini in Iran has also resulted in tension in Saudi Arabia and Kuwait. From a Western perspective, Shia is evolving into a more openly political religion, which would enforce new religious orthodoxy. To a devout Shiite, of course, Shia is only affirming the original religion of Ali, the cousin, son-in-law, and rightful heir of Mohammed.

The opposition to the reforming dynasty of the Pahlavis included a wide spectrum of the Iranian population, from Marxists to middle-class liberals. The religious leadership dominated the population however, and eventually prevailed in realizing some of the doctrine of governance by Islamic jurists, which Khomeini had urged in 1970.

Leaders of the Shiites had opposed the Shah since his land reform measures of 1960. By 1977 most segments of the population had deep grievances. Moojan Momen's analysis pointed to the Islamic jurists being alarmed by the reduction of their land and income. The Shah's own alternative religious leadership, in that he claimed religious authority and founded parallel religious institutions, infuriated the traditional leadership. Students were outraged by government control of the universities. The agricultural population was losing in the economic changes. Governmental corruption and inflation alienated the business classes.[7]

In the late 1970s the Shah was suffering from cancer and was unable to decisively act to end dissent as he had earlier. The Carter human rights policy also threatened to decrease United States support for the repressive regime. The ancient regime was trying to reform a traditional society, but the religious leadership of that society was also evolving into a more militant resistance to Western influence.

The revolution itself had many causes and several parties, but because the traditional religious leadership in its new militant form emerged triumphant, its role cannot be minimized as a factor.

Khomeini was one of several leading Shiite teachers and leaders. His imprisonment and exile magnified his role as a persecuted Shiite personage and led to the increase of his leadership. The death of his son at the hands of the Shah's secret police SAVAK contributed to his refusal to compromise. His union of politics and theology was complete and rooted in the central tenets of the historical origins of Shiism. The mythology of Shiite origins was turned against the Shiite dynasty of the Pahlavis and their American support.

It was the massacre of seventy or more students in the seminary city of Qumm on January 9, 1978, following President Carter's visit to support the Shah that unleashed the revolution itself. The students had been demanding the return of Khomeini, the opening of closed schools, and a return to the constitution.

From that day forward, demonstrations for the martyrs took place each forty days, and each demonstration produced more martyrs. The government was unable to resist the demonstrations on Moslem holidays and continued to kill those seeking political change and martyrdom. By October strikes were added to the tactics of the demonstrations and workers joined the religious revolution. The government could and did change its leadership and tried to counter the movement, but the religious leadership and the power of martyrdom were irresistible. The Western-trained and equipped army began to dissolve, contributing to the movement by either turning its weapons over to the revolutionaries or in many cases contributing to the fervor by increasing the number of martyrs. When Khomeini returned on February 1, 1979, the revolutions succeeded, he assumed power, and he began to put to work his theology of governance by Islamic law. [8]

The presence of white-clothed youth seeking martyrdom in the closing days of the revolution evoked the mythic origins of Shiism at the battle of Karbala in A.D. 680. Khomeini successfully transferred the stigma of the Umayyad dynasty to the Pahlavi dynasty and their Western supporters. This transfer combined with the suggestion that Khomeini the Imam in exile spoke for the hidden Imam who would return as the Twelfth Imam provided a religious ideology that was irresistible to the crowds to Twelver Shiite faithful.

Ruhollah Khomeini, as a teacher of Islamic theological students, had taught a doctrine of mysticism that obliterated the distinction between subject and object. [9] The mysticism had inculcated an all-or-nothing approach to politics, creating a sense of fearlessness, which was seen on the streets.

During the 1960s the mullahs or Islamic teachers had become more activist. Their political activity was set against the Westernizing tendencies of the Shah's regime. Their activities reached back to the historical myths of the origin of Shia or the party of Ali. Ali, according to Shia interpretations, was the person closest to the prophet Mohammed. He was the rightful heir, but his place was usurped by the Umayyads and then he was assassinated. The origins of this religious movement were political-religious. Ali was revered as the first Imam. His grandson Hosain was martyred along with his followers at the battle of Karbala in Iraq. The interpretations of Hosain as a religious martyr and a thwarted revolutionary are mixed in Shia interpretation. Khomeini and his followers used both interpretations against the Shah. The passions of Islamic theater combined with the religious holiday celebrations of the passion play to produce devotion to political struggle combined with martyrdom. Matthew Arnold compared accounts of the theater of Islam to the Oberammergau passion play in his essay "A Persian Passion Play" of 1871.[10]

This religious-political passion proved to be too much to resist for the Shah, who was treated as a religious usurper allied with Westerners who did not understand the Shia union of religion and politics. The same religious passion is expressed in the jihad or holy war with Iraq, which strives to unseat Iraq's government, to free the Shia majority population from heretical domination, and to regain the holy city of Karbala. Iraq's struggle to defend itself depends more on the government's ability to retain the loyalty of its Shia population than it does on Western weapons.

The adherents of the Shiite crusade to cleanse the Middle East of American and Israeli presence tend to believe:

(1) There is no separation of religion and politics,
(2) Islam should return to its fundamental beliefs,
(3) There should be no reliance on outsiders (infidels), and
(4) Shia should become even more active in expelling foreign powers.[11]

Since Napoleon conquered Egypt, Islam has, according to Shia perceptions, been humiliated by the West. This humiliation was deepened by Israel's victories in several wars. Only in the last war with Israel was it demonstrated that Moslems could fight Israel as an equal. The defeat of the Shah has breathed new hope into the consciousness of the Shia leaders that Western dominance can be broken and that Islam can return to purer roots.

A Christian Realist Response

The president of the United States in his apology for sending weapons to Iran discussed the geopolitical significance of the country. It meets the Persian Gulf on one side, it has an extensive border with the Soviet Union, and it meets Afghanistan on another side. Previous statements from the State Department have described Iran as an area of vital interest to the United States. Its potential as a supplier of oil to the West is recognized, as is the shrinking of that supply under Iraqi attack. The president has also affirmed a supposed Soviet interest in acquiring a warm-water seaport. It is known that the Soviets have practiced strategy for an invasion of Iran. This information of course does not answer the question of whether the supply of weapons to Khomeini's regime in Iran is a wise move. Certainly the United States has no interest in an Iranian victory in its war with Iraq or with strengthening its hand against moderate Arab allies who support Iraq.

There is no reason to suspect that the United States can have a helpful influence in ending the Iraq-Iran war. If Iraq cannot prevail, there is no reason to assist Iran in prevailing. Stalemate is preferable to a Khomeini victory from a U.S. perspective. There likewise would be no gain for the United States to prefer outstanding successes by Iraq that might involve a Soviet intervention. It is best to let the respective states tire of their futile bloodletting and to hope for more moderate leadership to eventually emerge in Iran, probably after Khomeini's death. The traditional warm-water port policy of Russia has usually meant influence in Istanbul and not the conquest of Iran. The indigestibility of Afghanistan must dissuade Soviet strategists from attempting to conquer Iran unless it falls apart. Even then the Soviet Union cannot rest assured that the United States would permit significant gains in Iran. Iran itself will resist the Soviet Union. A factor neglected by the Washington policy pronouncements is the significant religious interest in the fight against the West.

The United States policy would benefit from attempting to understand religious terrorism. The churches could play a significant role in this through interpreting religious terrorism, teaching about Islam, and holding forums on Iran's history, culture, religion, and politics. The growth of knowledge about an enemy helps us to understand and appreciate an enemy. A theology of peacemaking at the grass roots would help inform those who make policy of issues involved in dealing with organized religious-state terrorism.

The United States needs to learn the fact that terrorism is directed at policy and policy makers, and only indirectly if cruelly at the victims. It is not the residents of New Jersey who are attacked by terrorists, but the policy of directing the battleship New Jersey to fire into villages in Lebanon.

Islam has been humiliated for two centuries by the West. In Iran the American-sponsored Shah regime was the particular opponent of the Shia. So the United States is seen as both repulsive and attractive by Islam. It must struggle against the West for its own autonomy, the men could say for their manhood. But the attractions of technology and freedom are present too, as well as the Western-influenced minds of thousands of the educated elite who were trained and sometimes humiliated in Western universities.

Part of the United States' response to terrorism is to improve means of protecting U.S. citizens and interests. The program to strengthen embassies against attack makes sense. It is to be hoped never again will we leave Marines exposed to attack as they were in Beirut. The blunder of leaving sleeping Marines unprotected in a hostile area should never have happened. How is it that such an error did not result in prosecutions within the military and civilian command structure, which caused this loss? Young American lives cannot be put needlessly at such risk. Tougher security on airlines, including armed guards in regions threatened by terrorists, seems in order. If security at airports is inadequate, American planes should not be permitted to use the facilities. We cannot achieve complete security, but risks can be reduced.

Even without focusing on our negligence, we can make many efforts to decrease the danger. The literature on combating terrorism is full of discussions on better physical precautions, cautioning the news media, psychological toughening of Americans entering dangerous zones, new weapons, and new techniques of countering terrorism.

Economic sanctions, though morally easier to accept than military responses to terrorism, have not had much success. The policy of the United States of shipping arms to Iran while discouraging allies from trading with Iran has proved embarrassing. The possibilities of economic sanctions dissuading religious revolutionaries seem slight. Weapons and weapon-related technologies (e.g., plastic explosives) need to be kept away from terrorist countries, but the fluid, uncontrolled economic system seems unable to promise significant gains.

Consequently, military options must be considered. Just-war theory recognizes the appropriateness of punishing actors who attack representatives and citizens of sovereign nations. Terrorists do not receive immunity from attack. Military responses of a democracy informed by Christian morality require limitations. The military response must be proportional to the good to be achieved by such a response. This allows for significant military responses conducted under appropriate authority to discourage, possibly to stop, major terrorist campaigns. The attack must be discriminate; civilians not engaged in direct terrorism are immune from attack. Every effort must be made to protect civilians from direct U.S. attack. These moral considerations weigh heavily against using naval gunfire and air-bombing attacks, because the available evidence shows these weapons normally to be unable to discriminate in favor of civilians.

There are other options, but they too are limited by practical and moral considerations. It is difficult to use U.S. agents because they are so easily identifiable within the locales of the terrorists. The use of foreign nationals runs the risks of the recruited nationals carrying out their own designs and not the aims of the United States.

Even the successful killing of terrorists seems to encourage cults of martyrdom. Bombing attacks such as the ones on Libya tend to kill more children than terrorists, and to corrupt us morally when we resort to such tactics. They also violate international law and show little promise of ending terrorism. There are limits on U.S. response as a Christian informed democracy and they are set aside only at great cost to us.

What Is to Be Done?

We must avoid the solutions of both the soft utopians and the hard utopians. The hard utopians would try to attack plastic explosives in a suitcase with the sixth fleet. The religious conviction and willingness to suffer martyrdom means you cannot defeat these terrorists from the safety of the battleship New Jersey or the technological wonder of a fighter-bomber aircraft hurled half way around Europe. The soft utopians would tell us we must have effective world government and world courts with authority. This is foolishness because it is the very meaning of courts that is being fought over.

The realistic peacemaking way is to seek, gradually, a *rapproche-*

ment. The Ayatollah Khomeini will not live forever; even Stalin died. The United States and Iran will have years to work out their reconciliation. They were allies. The U.S. does not need Iran as a client state. They can, over time, recognize the dignity of each while retaining their reservations about the social organization of the other.

So we start private communication; words are central to the process of healing humiliated pride. We begin to disentangle ourselves from the mistakes of the Shah. When we cannot directly resolve the issues, we can have our allies move for us. Iran needs our nonmilitary technology and we begin to make it available on terms agreeable to both sides. We move in every way to treat Moslems as equals, ending their fear of subjugation. With more than 80 million believers, Shia must be recognized as a major world religion. Crusades run down and we can help the militancy run down by initiatives to reduce the pain.

Israel's existence is, of course, not negotiable, but a homeland for the Palestinians is, and our policies will need to support moderate Arab leaders and moderate Israeli leaders.

In short, in the face of provocation, we must protect ourselves, avoid the fanaticism of punishment or the illusion of fixing the world, seek negotiations, and cultivate the best tendencies in Iran and Islam. We learned in the failures of the Crusades of the Middle Ages that Islam is here to stay and we have to learn to live with it.

Robin Wright concludes her study:

> In the fourteenth century, Ibn Khaldun, a famous philosopher widely revered today in the Muslim world wrote that "Humanity's distinguishing characteristic is the ability to think . . . and through thinking to cooperate." The Koran itself demands of the faithful: "And if they incline towards peace, incline yourself also towards it."[12]

Three aspects of combating terrorism are particularly the work of the church. Most terrorists have a view of the world divided between the good and the evil. This heretical Manichaeism can be combated through better church communicating of theology and interreligiously through dialogues, conferences, and study.

The ability to recruit terrorists has its roots in the brutality experienced in the childhood of those recruited as terrorists.[13] All the relief work we can do to decrease the brutality of life in refugee camps and even to strengthen the quality of life for our own brutalized American children will help to dry up the roots of terrorism, American or Palestinian.

The third task of the church is to teach its members its own traditions about the use of force. The crusade tradition has been found to be inadequate, which leaves the pacifist tradition and the justifiable-unjustifiable war tradition as the two options. The teaching of the justifiable-unjustifiable war tradition will help Christians understand why terroristic violence must be rejected as immoral.[14] Though apologists for terrorism will try to justify their actions, there are no adequate avenues of reasoning to that end. Inasmuch as the just-war tradition of the Western philosophical and religious tradition has been universalized in the United Nations Charter, in treaties, and in rulings of international law, terrorism is immoral and illegal. It cannot pass, ordinarily, the requirement that violence be originated by a legitimate authority. It intentionally violates the prohibition against attacks on noncombatants. It is generally unable to achieve its goals of political change. The requirement of right attitudes for the conduct of war is regularly violated by known terrorists. The need to defend just order does not usually seem to be met by terrorist groups. The moral case against condoning most forms of terrorism is clear. The tradition of justifiable war also limits the response of the United States. Obviously, bombing attacks on cities is proscribed morally by our own methods of moral reasoning.

The typical defense of terrorism has been to call it a method of war of the weak against the strong. There is a plausible argument that terrorism does not neglect the need to protect civilians any more than other wars of the twentieth century. Ali A. Mazrui writes in defense of terrorism: "No one on the side of the Allies worried about how many German civilians were killed in Dresden or Berlin as the two cities were pulverized in the closing stages of World War II. . . . Civilian casualties ceased to be a major worry of the twentieth-century warfare decades ago."[15]

However, he is mistaken, first factually and then morally. Many, including Christian realists, spoke out against targeting civilians and against the obliteration style of Allied warfare. Second, moral reasons cannot be given for violating the humanity of noncombatants. The fact that morality has been violated is no moral justification for further immorality. Terrorism, nuclear deterrence, and the bombing of cities all fail because of their attempt to achieve political aims through terrorizing noncombatants.

A fourth task of the church is to begin the dialogue with Shia. In the Islamic affirmation of the Mosaic and prophetic traditions including

Jesus, we have a basis for dialogue. Our common heritage of Aristotelian philosophy also opens up possibilities. Max Stackhouse, writing on terrorism, points to the need for transcultural norms.[16] We have the beginnings in our common but too often neglected heritage. The mullah leadership of Iran has often favored constitutional government, which is a necessary prerequisite for the defense of human rights. Through dialogue and mutual education we can help strengthen Iranian developments toward constitutional government, and we can learn how our foreign policy toward Iran often contributes to suppressing human rights.

IX. RELATIONS WITH THE RUSSIANS

A ll reflections on the ethics of peacemaking by Americans must grapple with the question, What about the Russians? The issue is raised in various ways. Political philosophers have discussed it under the exploration of superpower ethics.[1] Critics of church programs in peacemaking have attacked mainline-church programs as teaching a doctrine of the "moral equivalence" of the Soviet Union and the United States.[2] The question is often raised after discussing Central American, South African, or Middle Eastern concerns as if to imply all peacemaking founders on the hard reality of Soviet competition. The question is fundamental to the differing policy recommendations for U.S. policy from hard-line neoconservative thinkers like Richard Pipes and Christian realists like George Kennan.[3]

Realism about the Russians requires noting that their traditions are very different from ours. They are a Euro-Asian people with different religious traditions and different philosophical traditions than Western European-American civilization. A Russian crowd celebrating their victory over Nazism in Red Square may look physically a lot like a state fair crowd in Des Moines, Iowa. However their minds have been molded by experience different from ours. They have a thousand-year history of Greek Christianity, which has evolved quite differently from Roman Christianity and its Reformation heirs. They do not have the same independence from the state in religious matters that has characterized American Christianity. The philosophies of Locke, Montesquieu, Madison, Jefferson, and Smith have not been institutionalized in their social structure as they have in ours. The tradition of human rights honored in their constitution and the Helsinki accords has not been embodied in their governmental practice. The Marxist goals of establishing socialism and evolving into

151

Communism, which guide their moral thinking, are absent from our minds. Our development into a Western-Christian mixed economy with great political liberties is radically different from their Orthodox history and their state-socialist economy.

They have known Western philosophies and experienced some Western Christianity just as we have known some socialist impulses and absorbed millions of Orthodox Christians, but basically their ethos is different. Although we have been allied against Nazism, our experience of World War II was different. Their recovery from the war without our assistance has left them dominating most of the pre–World War I Czarist empire as well as some additions. Our emergence from World War II, which never really threatened our homeland, left us in a dominant position in the world outside the socialist bloc. Marxist ethics and Christian ethics are not the same, our historical experience is not the same. Consequently, the neoconservatives charge that the realists' assertion, a moral equivalence of the Soviet Union and the United States, is silly. We cannot be morally equivalent because our moral systems are radically different. The goals of the Soviet Union differ substantially from the goals of the United States, and the principles by which they evaluate their moral life also differ. The evolution toward a parliamentary government under the Czars, which Richard Pipes among others has noted, was cut off in its infancy. Their history has been one of totalitarianism, radically different from the liberal democratic trends of the Western world. To the extent that state socialism especially under Lenin and Stalin tried actively to change human nature it has been in direct moral clash with the Western tendency to try to adjust government to the pluralistic expression of human nature.

The realist approach has been to severely criticize cruelties of the Soviet Union, to balance potential military power with power, to hope for a waning of the more militant aspects of Soviet ambitions, and to try to help the United States patiently exert its responsibilities as one of two superpowers. Kennan's criticism of the Soviet Union resulted in his being expelled from the Soviet Union from his post as ambassador. Niebuhr's criticism of the Soviet Union led many to criticize him as overly hawkish. Morgenthau's reliance on the balancing-of-power approach led him to be rejected as some sort of Machiavellian. All of those have come to see and to emphasize that the present need was to tame the military competition and to manage the nuclear terror. Niebuhr expressed this in a comment about Kennan:

It was the chairman of that group, George Kennan who first formulated the policy of the containment of Communism in the famous Mr. X article in *Foreign Affairs* (July, 1947), but I think we've all followed him in shifting away from the containment of Communism to the partnership of the two superpowers for the prevention of a nuclear war. This is the change that history has wrought, so that Kennan would be the first one now to disavow any simple containment of Communism.[4]

Realism has moved away from a simple military containment of Communism, but that does not mean a forswearing of military responses to Communism where appropriate. It means that the partnership for managing the nuclear weaponry has a priority. It means that in some situations, such as Vietnam, a military response is inappropriate after the French loss of their colony. It does not mean unilateralism in disarmament; it does not mean abandoning NATO, or a premature disengagement from other military responsibilities like the honoring of commitments in Korea.

Before we examine the opportunities for partnership in the Gorbachev era, reflection on the last forty years of neither peace nor world war is appropriate. A marvelous dialogue between high-ranking Russian political leaders and interpreters and American political leaders and intellectuals was held at the University of Texas in April of 1986. The late arrival of some of the Soviet delegation and the preponderance of Americans present skewed the discussion somewhat; however, the presentations and discussion in the seminar provide perspective on this period of tension.[5]

More Than Forty Years Without World War

Neither the Soviet Union nor the United States intends to fight a war with the other. The cold war seems to be stabilizing as the superpowers approach the end of the third millennium. (War between the two appeared to be a greater risk at mid-century than it does as we approach the end of the century.) Two major developments reinforce this conclusion. One represents a gain by the Soviet Union and the other a gain by the United States. The first factor is that the Soviet Union has achieved a rough parity in weapons of mass destruction with the United States. This was achieved in the 1960s. The Soviet Union can feel relatively secure from an attack by the United States. Andrey A. Kokoshin has expressed this security from a Soviet perspective: "In my view, our feeling of security now is greatest since maybe the times of Peter the Great."[6] Similarly, parity means the United States, though vulnerable, need fear no rational attack from the Soviet Union. There can be no rational calculation of waging war; the enormity and rough parity of the weapons prevent rational planning for war.

The second factor is the waning of the attractiveness of the Soviet model of socialism for the developing nations. Russian influence in the developing nations has declined since the 1960s. The withdrawal of China from the Soviet sphere of influence has been accompanied by the decline of Soviet influence in India and Indonesia. This decline of influence in the first, second, and fifth most populous countries in the world has been a decisive setback to any Soviet dreams of world leadership. In the 1950s Americans could fear that the Soviet Union's socialism might look attractive to the rest of the world. But the developments of the following years saw countries in Africa, for example, Egypt, Somalia, and Ghana, reject Soviet advances. True, others like Angola, Libya, and Ethiopia tilted toward the Soviet Union, but the resoluteness of others in rejecting Soviet advances indicated there was no African drifted toward Soviet socialism. Elsewhere in the world in the 1980s there seemed to be a drift toward democracy and away from authoritarian models of government. John Lewis Gaddis, commenting on the decline of the Soviet socialist movement, noted both its splintering and its reverses.

> When we Americans become concerned, as we often do about the spread of communism in the Third World, we fail to realize that the unity and appeal of the movement have severely declined. In this sense, I think it is possible to argue that indeed we've won the Cold War, and we won it a long time ago.[7]

So we now live in a world of rough parity in weaponry between the superpowers in which the attractiveness of the model of the Soviet revolutionary power has declined.

Relevant to the question of the stability of the rivalry between the Soviet Union and the United States are two other factors. The first is the economic recovery of Western Europe and Japan since the 1950s. The economies of these democracies all are more productive than that of the Soviet Union. Their alliance with the world's greatest economy in the United States makes Soviet predictions of the economic collapse of the West appear to be only loyalty to old-fashioned Marxist dreams.[8] Still, such predictions in Gorbachev and the Communist Party program are all set within the quest for a durable peace. The other factor relevant to the question of a stable rivalry is the relative instability of the Soviet sphere of influence. The wag who asked which country is the only one surrounded by hostile Communist powers was not far wrong when he answered himself with "Russia." Rumania refused to follow the Soviet Union's foreign policy line, and Hungary, Czechoslovakia, East Germany, and Poland are kept in line by force. Afghanistan is relatively indigestible. China is hostile. Mongolia and North Korea alone of the Soviet's neighbors seem subdued. The Central-Eastern European question remains a potential threat to the stability of the rivalry.

Some credit to the umbrella of terror of the weapons of mass destruction must be given for the more than forty years of no world war. The umbrella of terror, of course, has not prevented the world from having more than one hundred non-nuclear wars. The very development of technology, which is the foundation of the terror that has given some stability, is also destabilizing. Negotiators for arms control note that the technological developments can outstrip the pace of negotiations, rendering the process even more difficult. The threats of technological discoveries that could upset the rough parity are also destabilizing.

The recognition that the Soviet Union's and United States' mutually antagonistic weapons systems are together one system, which has deterred conflict from becoming all-out war, still does not permit acceptance of the system. The dangers of the failure of the system are too great if one side were to be forced into unacceptable losses in the competition. The system would become more unstable if one of the major powers were to decline while the other grew. There is a possibility, though small, of inadvertent war owing to technical or human mistakes. Conventional war in sensitive areas could escalate too rapidly for controls to prevent nuclear war. The present expense of the system robs the world of technological and economic resources, which justice demands be used to relieve suffering. Finally, as argued in the chapter on justifiable war, deterrence through threatening omnicide or even through threatening noncombatants is immoral by the same processes of thought that makes defense moral. Morality requires the careful, mutual, negotiated moving away from the system of deterrence based on the threat of civilian destruction.

The Era of Gorbachev

The goal of the policy of containment articulated forty years ago was "the gradual mellowing of Soviet power." Kennan regarded it as improbable that a messianic political movement could face frustration indefinitely without adjusting to reality.[9] The frustrations of the Soviet Union on the international side have been noted. Equally relevant to the emergence of new directions are the frustrations on the social-economic side. New directions in Soviet policy are arising from these dual pressures. These pressures and the new leadership of the Soviet Union may provide, as W. W. Rostow suggests, an opportunity for ending the cold war.[10]

The rise to prominence of a new group of economists in the Soviet Union provides a clue to the real aim of Gorbachev's changes. Abel G. Aganebegyan, Oleg T. Bogomolov, Leonid J. Abalkin, and Tatyano Zaslavskaya under Gorbachev's leadership are developing plans for market economy within the socialist system of the Soviet Union.[11] Aganebegyan's urging of the downgrading of centralized economic control and price regulation would have been heretical before Gorbachev, but now he is the chief economic advisor to the government. The possibility of this change developed in the closing years of Brezhnev as more and more leaders perceived stagnation and declining vitality in the Soviet system of production. Much of the Soviet leadership consequently has been prepared for *perestroika*, or restructuring of the economy.[12] The growth rate in the economy has declined in the 1980s until 1985, and the Soviet system has seemed unable to produce goods and services of sufficient quality and quantity to meet the public demand. The workforce has seemed dispirited and not as productive as is desirable. Most observers view Soviet society as rather backward and underdeveloped compared to its immediate neighbors of Finland, East Germany, and Hungary. On a trip on the Trans-Siberian Express in 1983 in Central Asia, I myself observed the irony of bills being calculated with an abacus while porters displayed their Texas Instrument, solar powered calculators.

Soviet technology has been very good where it has received sufficient priorities, but the economy as a whole remains mired in a bureaucracy, using semiprimitive approaches to production. The results have been leaving much of the countryside (even that visible on a tourist-traveled route like the Trans-Siberian Express) looking like an undeveloped frontier. The problems show up even in favored

Moscow, where state officials in unguarded moments complain about the lack of food in the stores. But beyond the observable primitiveness and consumer shortages, the government itself admits the economy is not doing well and that incentives must be built into the system to rejuvenate it.

Coming into power with Gorbachev is a generation fifteen years younger than their predecessors, as seen in the Politburo and Secretariat. They are a "blend of technocratic types and enforcers" according to the analysis of George W. Breslauer.[13] They are party people raised within a philosophy of central planning. Many of them are personnel experts. They are people who can help Gorbachev build a machine and follow his leadership as long as it promises success. With his new economists he has ideas, and with his recruited followers from the provinces he has managers. He seems to be lacking, when compared to Brezhnev, close ties with the military and the old-guard network, which could protect him if he stumbled badly. Economic-social change is perceived as needed; if his economic reshuffling can succeed, he probably has a bright future in the Soviet Union. At his relatively young age, he could be guiding the Soviet Union until A.D. 2000 and beyond.

The Soviet Union's dependence on foreign trade is rather modest, about 6 percent of G.N.P. Even so, the prospects for improvement here are not great. The Soviet Union can supply raw materials and energy resources, but it still depends on the West for advanced technology and supplementary food supplies. The emergence of high-technology centers in the Pacific, Europe, and the United States raises doubts about the ability of the Soviet Union to compete internationally in advanced machinery and technologically sophisticated consumer goods. Much of the Soviet Union's economic development will depend on the growth of internal markets, and this again turns back to the development of the Soviet producer and consumer.

Wassily Leontief, a winner of the 1973 Nobel Memorial Prize in Economic Science, has cautioned those in the West who dream of the emergence of capitalism in the Soviet Union to remember the small interest in reform among the workers.[14] The workers have security and they have constantly been taught of the insecurities and hardships of Western economy. Another problem in adjustment is the fact of a large underclass of people in the Soviet Union, who would suffer under the rise in the basic cost of living that a market-oriented price structure would cause. Rise in prices of basic commodities have been central to social disturbances, riots, and unrest in the socialist states of Eastern Europe. Gorbachev has been fortunate in the sudden growth of the economy in 1986 up to a 4.1 percent rise in G.N.P. The gain mostly depends on higher prices for oil and a good harvest, but politicians thrive on such coincidences, and it strengthens his hand at an opportune moment.

Licensing of small private enterprises, decentralization of investment decisions, increased incentives for production, increased autonomy for farms, increased private production of agricultural products, and a campaign against inefficient managers do not in themselves mean the end of socialism. But they certainly increase freedom for limited economic decision making and this disperses some power. These gains and promised gains in economic freedom are matched by increased freedom in the cultural and even political sphere. Of course such gains are limited by Western standards, but to the extent that Western requirements for deemphasizing the cold war have included cultural and political freedoms in the Soviet Union, something significant is happening.

Traveling in the Soviet Union in 1983, I was aware of the exile in Gorky of Sakharov and thousands of other prisoners. His release and his support for Gorbachev's move toward *glasnost*, "openness," or perhaps better, "speaking out," inspired hope that the atrocities of the gulag might be coming to an end. The reality of the gulag as described so movingly by Aleksandr Solzhenitsyn has prevented bolder American moves toward peacemaking with the Soviet Union. Under Stalin and to a lesser degree Khrushchev, the Soviet Union had been governed by terror. American responses to the Soviet Union mix concerns for freedom and for a just peace. The suppression of human rights by starvation, imprisonment, and murder has simply thwarted American movements toward peace.

The breaking of the Helsinki Human Rights support group under Brezhnev cast a pallor over the Western peace movements. Some peace activists could look away from this violation of the Helsinki accords. But the peace movement had a harder time winning support because of the suppression in the Soviet Union. To a degree, the emergence of the dissentors from the prisons, the camps, and the asylums will encourage the peace movement in the West. Will human rights advocacy groups be allowed to regroup?

Religious supporters of the peace movements will also be awaiting the end of religious persecution. Solzhenitsyn's descriptions of dissenting Baptists in the camps are imbedded in minds that will not be able to seek the normalization of relations until the antireligious harassment is ended. Similar concerns for Seventh Day Adventists, Jews, and other persecuted religious groups will thwart peacemaking until their rights are recognized.

There is religious persecution in the Soviet Union. Believers are not free to establish churches, proselytize, teach, and act as their religious beliefs motivate them. Thousands of believers have been killed because of their Christian identity; thousands more have been systematically imprisoned; most of the religious population has been discriminated against as positions of power in society are reserved for atheists. So the religious community in the Western world will need to see a lot of evidence of liberalization and religious tolerance to be persuaded that the Soviet Union is becoming serious about human rights.

Western observers of the Soviet Union generally report seeing full churches. That has been my own experience. I have also observed women praying in buildings that were formerly churches, but which are now called museums. But thousands of church buildings have been closed. The monastic system, one of the great glories of Old Russia, has been destroyed with only a few permitted to resume the monastic life. The crowds filling the few churches are evidence of a faith that will not die, but also evidence of the few churches remaining for worship. Some of Khrushchev's reforms were accompanied by a persecution of the church. The religious community still awaits evidence of new policy toward the church for the Gorbachev era.

Toleration of the marvelous creativity of the human spirit is seen in a new openness toward a variety of cultural and artistic expressions. Films formerly banned are being shown. New art and music are tolerated. Books formerly denounced and prohibited are now being published and read. The intellectual community is being courted by the new policies and they are responding favorably.

The limits of openness are not yet perceived. Western toleration of almost everything should not be anticipated as a policy of the Communist Party of the Soviet Union. There will be limits, but where they will be enforced is unclear. The Russian intellectual community can be counted on to push the limits in their creativity and criticism of the society. In the summer of 1987, Sergei Grigoryants was testing the limits. Only released from prison in the preceding February, after spending ten years incarcerated, he was trying to publish *Glasnost*, a journal of social, artistic, religious, economic, and political commentary.[15] Its fate will signal where the limits of creativity are to be placed.

Foreign and Military Policy

The United States is being challenged in its dominating world role by the activism of the Soviet Union. Bolstered by an increasing military strength, the Soviet Union has been seeking more influence in world affairs.

Under Gorbachev the military buildup continues as it has under Reagan's leadership. The Defense Department publication *Soviet Military Power, 1987* is sobering reading for all in the Western world who are engaged in peace movements.[16] Statistics from the Arms Control and Disarmament Agency show the Warsaw Pact nations keeping a greater percent of their population in military service and spending a greater proportion of their national income for the military than the NATO alliance.[17] The total spending by NATO is greater than that of the Warsaw group, although Warsaw maintains an edge in people in military service. The 1983 figures, which have been reasonably stable for a period of time, were 5,587,000 in service in NATO and 5,810,000 in Warsaw. Neither the numbers in service nor budgets are really comparable because of the different social systems and not too much weight should be placed in them.

Neither the armed forces in numbers nor the military budgets of NATO and the Warsaw Pact show a great advantage of one over the other. The potential deployment of NATO with its population advantage of roughly 3 to 2 and its G.N.P. advantage of 4 to 1 is, of course, much greater than that of Warsaw.

A more sobering use of the numbers supplied by the Department of Defense is that the two alliances contain more than 11,000,000 fighting personnel.[18] Can two competitive alliances build up the combined forces of nuclear, chemical, biological, and conventional forces aimed at each other and not use them? How long can the tension hold? After 145 pages of relatively detailed analysis of Soviet military power, the document then briefly in 14 pages summarizes the American buildup in the last eight years. That buildup across several systems is also frightening.

Gorbachev's diplomatic and peace offensive takes place in the middle of all of this recent Soviet modernization and buildup. Part of the situation is also a very anti-Communist administration in the United States. Gorbachev also inherits a war in Afghanistan, which he will not lose militarily but in which victory is nearly impossible. In late 1987 movement toward Soviet withdrawal from Afghanistan seemed promising.

He has allies in Angola and Ethiopia, which seem unable to prevail against Western-assisted liberation movements. In Nicaragua, he has to avoid all-out United States intervention while trying to assist a revolutionary-socialist government, which could become an ally. Other than military hardware, the world does not seem interested in purchasing many Russian products. Cuba is a negative factor viewed economically, but its troops are needed to sustain Soviet Third World strategies. The specter of the tightening encirclement of the Soviet Union by NATO, Pakistan, China, Japan, and the United States leaves him few options. The very expensive armed forces have few uses other than maintaining the East European satellites, trying to control Afghanistan, and preserving the Soviet Union's defense. On the other hand, no one is about to attack the Soviet Union anyway.

His options are largely diplomatic and military assistance. In arming Syria, Iraq, and India he can make it more difficult for the U.S. allies of Israel and Pakistan. Meanwhile he can attempt to sow dissension among U.S. allies with peace proposals, which may reveal their different national interests. He can hope to break the embargoes on high technology and he can hope to carry out some modernization with Western credit if he doesn't appear too threatening. He knows military threats are unbelievable against the U.S.-NATO forces, and he knows that war is unthinkable.

However, the United States, which has been rebuilding its military, has not been in a position from which it would wish to slow down its development. The team of foreign policy and military advisers around Reagan, and the president himself, were skeptical about arms control agreements. The United States set aside the honoring of SALT II and began to attack the ABM treaty, which the Soviets themselves violated with the new radar. The United States Strategic Defense Initiative seemed to set the United States on course to at least catch up with if not surpass Russian research into defense against ICBMs.[19] Diplomatic probing by the Soviet Union revealed the United States was in early 1988 unwilling to curtail its accelerated program in research for a missile defense.

The immediate opening for some retreat from the arms race has been in the area of intermediate and short-range nuclear missiles. Soviet advantages in this area in total numbers were negotiable with the United States and NATO, since the zero option required greater Russian dismantling of weapons. Possible Soviet gains could be seen in reducing one part of the U.S. deterrent in Europe where Russia possessed greater conventional strength on the ground. The other advantage to Gorbachev was in removing possible first-strike weapons so close to the Soviet Union. For the United States it promises to achieve the longtime goal of eliminating the SS20 threat to Europe.

The signing of the treaty in late 1987 began the process of eliminating 2,001 nuclear missiles. It is a major achievement to be received thankfully and realistically. An estimate of its significance awaits developments toward significant reductions in nuclear and other weapons of mass destruction and of increased accord in superpower relations. I received the news of the Geneva, Shultz-Shevardnadze agreement in Prague in a global seminar for peace, which included East European Christians, Third World participants, and Marxists. The response of the seminar was to applaud and to continue looking for moral foundations for world reconciliation.

Gorbachev's position as the initiator of the peace offensive portrayed him very favorably to the embattled President Reagan, who seemed too ready to use military options. Of course, Gorbachev's initiatives also offered Reagan the opportunity to achieve the public high-ground by agreement. Polls following the signing of the treaty revealed great support for President Reagan's dealings with the Soviet Union.

President Reagan, whose early judgments of the Soviet Union were formed in reaction to U.S. policy vis-à-vis Stalin, brought with him to power a group of persons deeply distrustful of the Soviet Union. With policies informed by neoconservative anti-Communism, they have had to confront the administrations of four different General Secretaries. The speed of the Gorbachev revolution has made it difficult to evaluate in time to respond. At the end of 1987 it was too soon to judge adequately the depth of the Gorbachev changes or their staying power. Also to be considered is that the Contra-Iran debacle tore apart the administration of national security policy within the White House, and many of the hardest-liners had left the government by the date of the treaty signing. Great opportunities may have been missed; some minor reductions in one form of nuclear terror have been achieved.

Mikhail Gorbachev's 1987 book *Perestroika* reveals his passion for getting the disarmament process and improvements in relations with the United States moving forward. [20] Beneath the propaganda qualities of the book, which was written for Western consumption, is the reality of a new leader who knows that nuclear war will end humanity. He knows that neither Russia nor socialism will dominate the world. As a humanist and an activist he is eager to begin backing down from the arms race.

The book is an apology for Soviet policies in the world and an appeal for understanding of his *perestroika*, or the restructuring of Soviet society program. The book is less provincial than previous writings of Soviet leaders. It is more international, more humanist, less rigidly socialist, and less narrowly Russian.

The subtitle of the book, *New Thinking for Our Country and the World*, is boldly new in calling for 50 percent reduction in nuclear forces and movement toward reducing terror. In international politics he abandons ideological politics to speak instead of the interests of nations. He is willing to recognize the interests of other nations and hopes that the United States will reciprocate. To the extent that beneath the rhetoric a soberminded peacemaker can be perceived, his presence at the head of the Soviet Union bodes well for reducing tensions and arms, if U.S. leadership is foresighted enough to deal realistically with him.

Western readers will find sections of the book unconvincing. The horrors of Soviet Russian history have not been faced honestly. Many sections of the book deal with salient topics too generally to be significant. The discussions of women's rights, ethnic rights, and ecological policy seem crude and underdeveloped. However his actions have already undergirded in a persuasive way the commitments to restructure the economy and to change relations with the United States, which are detailed in the book.

Uncertainties dominate the current state of U.S.-Soviet relations. From a perspective of Christian realism, grounding an ethic in faith, hope, and love, and seeking a just peace while aware of the Soviet Union reflected in *Soviet Military Power, 1987* and the *Gulag Archipelago*,[21] we can see some guidelines emerge:

(1) Patient and careful diplomacy committed to a goal of a just peace and the need for reducing the immoral terror must seek bilateral agreements in arms control and disarmament.

(2) The United States needs to radically increase its study, knowledge, and understanding of the Soviet Union.

(3) Despite their frustrations, American initiatives for travel to the Soviet Union, Soviet travel to the United States and dialogue must be increased.

(4) Business opportunities need to be sought to increase U.S.-Soviet accord.

(5) Openness in the Soviet Union can be welcomed, celebrated, and encouraged and the increase of human rights there urged.

(6) American provocative actions, policies, and rhetoric need to be replaced by patient firmness.

(7) U.S. policies encouraging democracy even when it has a socialist caste need to be firmly held.

Such policies in themselves will not achieve the illusive goal of a just peace, but they will move us closer to it and away from confrontation.

Relations with the Soviets ought to be based on the search for a just peace. This requires that the United States as a superpower with imperial responsibilities use force. The force must be limited and subject to the rules of the justifiable war tradition. The value of peace is overreaching, but as applied by policies of peacemaking, which in a world society in which the structures of order are feeble, force will be required. If the Soviet Union is mellowing domestically and perhaps in the area of weapons of mass destruction, the response of the United States can move closer and closer to higher standards of moral policy. The mutual dissolution of nuclear terror can begin. If less military expenditure can be achieved policies for greater American domestic economic justice can be advanced. Less conflict in the developing world would permit greater investment in economic development in the poor societies of the planet. The backdown from the militarization of the planet under cold war pressures would benefit all societies, even the arms exporting economies, in the long run. Partnership for the development of the world is probably a utopian expectation between two powers as economically and ideologically diverse as the Soviet Union and the United States. But partnership in reducing the threat of annihilation is realistic, and it provides opportunities for world development.

X. TOWARD A RELEVANT CHURCH POLICY

Church policy is the theory and action of Christian faith in relation to the daily life and priorities of the church. The church lives in both its gathered communities of worship, education, planning, and action, and in its scattered life of Christian participation in the world's economy, voluntary associations, and governing institutions. Church policy is focused on both the church itself as a peacemaking community and Christians themselves acting in the world as peacemakers. Retreat into an emphasis on the church itself as peacemaker misunderstands that Christians live both in the church itself and in the world. Focusing solely on Christian engagement in the world neglects the formative power of Christian community. Peacemaking in the church is for the world, for God's world.

Initiatives toward peacemaking ministries have spread throughout the denominations in the United States. One of the most interesting efforts has been the United Church of Christ's declaration of itself as a just-peace church. This policy, which is to be put into effect throughout the structures of the church, represents a move from the traditional just-war theologies toward the harnessing of just-peace theologies and structures. In opposition to the institution of war, the church has begun defining the meaning of just peace as the interrelation of friendship, justice, and common security.

The policy presupposes a rather complete outline of theological priorities affirming the traditional marks of Christian realist analysis and the newer emphases of peacemaking. The inseparability of peace and justice is a theme as is the search for basic, mutual security among nations. The policy is also characterized by a sharp rejection of nuclear deterrence policy and doctrine. The need for congregational support of persons who engage in nonviolent civil disobedience to

165

witness against specific military actions of the governments is affirmed.

Many other denominations are also deepening their peacemaking commitments. This concluding chapter explores how local churches may put into action policies of peacemaking.

A Variety of Churches

The consideration of Christian policy in peacemaking focuses first on the local churches. Not all local churches are equally prepared to participate in a peacemaking ministry. The congregations and their leadership must be met where they live and led into the deeper realms of peacemaking. Though each congregation is different, it is helpful to think of congregations as consisting of three types. As Augustine taught us a long time ago, all people seek peace, and the differences reside in the meanings of peace they pursue and in their means to achieve these goals.

The first type may be regarded as the *Peace as Present* church. In this congregation, peace often has two meanings. It means peace of the inner self with God, and it also means deterring war with strength. This congregation tends to trust in deterrence, honors the military, and tends to regard the maintenance of the peace as primarily the task of the government. The congregation may also tend to regard Communism as an absolute enemy of Christianity. There are peacemaking activities that would be wholly inappropriate to attempt in a congregation of the *Peace as Present* type. However, there are many actions that are appropriate in this type of congregation.

(1) Biblical study of the meaning of *shalom* is always appropriate. Every denomination is preparing biblical study materials on peace. Representative resources include Donald Gowan, *Shalom: A Study of the Biblical Message Concerning Peace*; John Howard Yoder, *The Politics of Jesus*; essays by Lamar Williamson, George Edwards, Donald Gowan, and Ulrich Mauser in Ronald Stone and Dana Wilbanks (eds.), *The Peacemaking Struggle*; and Walter Brueggemann, *Living Toward a Vision: Biblical Reflections on Shalom*.

(2) Study of peace in other religious traditions can open up perspectives and is ordinarily welcome in the church. Two new volumes that are helpful are Mark Jurgensmeyer, *Fighting with Gandhi*, which examines Gandhi and the Indian religious background, and Annette Dawn and Eugene Fisher, *The Challenge of*

Shalom for Catholics and Jews. K. G. Saryidain's *Islam, the Religion of Peace* predates the new Islamic militancy, but is very helpful.

(3) The meaning of "Love your enemy" can be explored by studying literature on the theology of the enemy. See essays by Barbara Green and Robert Smylie in Ronald Stone and Dana Wilbanks (eds.), *The Peacemaking Struggle.* General courses on the Soviet Union and Marxism can usually be taught in adult forum sessions.

(4) Most churches can respond to courses on the history of the just-war teaching and alternatives to the just-war position. The historical presentations will evoke questions for our day even if the teachers do not specifically examine the present military alternatives. Roland Bainton's *Christian Attitudes Toward War and Peace,* is the classic text for the teacher or the class. Paul Ramsey, *War and the Christian Conscience,* and James Turner Johnson, *Just War Tradition and the Restraint of War* complement and provide alternative readings of the tradition to Bainton.

(5) Youth programs can be developed to show how Christian faith leads to a personal sense of purpose for the common good. Vocational discussions are needed to help the young people examine the trajectories of their lives. Youth can be sent to institutes and program activities on peacemaking that this type of local congregation would not host itself. The youth particularly need to experience the creativity of the broader ecumenical church.

(6) The work of promoting justice through development of human resources can flourish in this type of congregation. Aid for Africa and Central American can be raised, and the fundraising opportunities provide opportunity for mission education. Mission programs provide one of the best opportunities for broadening the horizons of Americans in this type of church.

The second type is the *Peace as Program* church. The leadership of this type of congregation is more concerned about the dangers of war than the first type. They tend not to trust so thoroughly the ability to maintain peace through military strength. This congregation already has an established nucleus of laypersons working consciously on peace issues. In some cases the lay peace group receives the support of the pastor; in others the pastor only tolerates the peace group. This congregation can do all of the educational and mission-oriented work of the *Peace as Present* church, but it can go farther. The *Peace as Program* church, though concerned about the world, characteristically focuses its energies inward on the congregation. In going further this type of congregation can:

(7) Involve educational speakers and books that specifically analyze the war-peace issues, including an analysis of the Soviet and American systems. The criteria of the just war and movement for a just peace can be applied to decision making. Alan Geyer's *The Idea of Disarmament*, or Richard Barnet's *The Roots of War*, or George Kennan's *The Nuclear Delusion* are all political analyses of a high order by Christian peacemakers.

(8) Some congregations of this type are ready to examine the use of their financial resources for peacemaking. Most denominations have materials on the ethics of investment for peacemaking. It is appropriate and exciting for the ethical issues of investment in corporations deeply involved in South Africa or armaments to be acted on by the governing bodies of congregations.

(9) The competition for funds and energy of the social welfare aspects of American and international society over against the cost of armaments is appropriate for church programming here. The evocation and deepening of social justice needs is always appropriate both in its own terms and as a counter to the militarization of society's priorities. Even though this type of congregation might not take an ethical-political stand itself, it can encourage the members in their continuing reformation of the social structures in which they are responsible.

(10) These congregations can be lead to understand and to appreciate the truths in liberation theologies from the developing world countries, American minorities, and women. Through study, attitudes toward revolution and counterrevolution can be changed. Black theology compels whites to understand the injustice of the American system. The literature and speakers of women's liberation expose the most widespread oppression, the oppression of women by men. The liberation theologies express the human struggle for development and human rights and thereby contribute to *shalom*. Alan Boesak's *Farewell to Innocence* and Gustavo Gutiérrez's *The Power of the Poor in History* express respectively the struggle for liberation in South Africa and Latin America. Rosemary Ruether's *Liberation Theology* unites the movements as well as any study. James Cone's *God of the Oppressed* represents the anguish and the power of American black theology. Most of the members of these churches

may not identify in solidarity with these concerns, but they can have their sensitivities transferred so that they can support the movements.

(11) In these churches the women of the church are the more thoroughly educated in the theologies of development and liberation because their women's associations have been working on these issues for years. The sensitivities of the women are more developed than those of the men both because of this education, and also because of their different roles toward war. War for men has produced romance, community, and adventure as well as suffering. For American women, war has meant deprivation and the loss of husbands, brothers, and children with few compensations. The training in the glorification of violence has not been able to penetrate the reality of women as thoroughly as it has men. Consequently women's energies are dominant in the peace movements. The injustices of gender oppression have also left men more exposed to the pressures of daily work in the military-industrial complex, and so their reluctance to identify themselves with peace movements is increased. The witness of several women is recorded in Jim Wallis' *The Peacemakers*, and the urgency of the peace issue is caught in the several dynamic books by Dorothee Soelle, including *The Arms Race Kills*. Central to the development of these *Peace as Program* churches is the empowerment of the women's groups to provide leadership for the whole church. The women will as a group support actions in the boards, sessions, and consistories of congregations that their husbands will reject. Consequently, achieving proportional representation in the governance of the churches contributes to Christian peacemaking. This recognition of women's leadership in the church encourages the implications of *shalom* for our church politics and priorities. Women must be freed from the church's kitchens and bazaars to address the true needs of the church. Paul put it well in writing to the newly formed church in Rome nineteen hundred years ago:

> The kingdom of God is not eating and drinking, but *justice, peace,* and joy inspired by the Holy Spirit. (Romans 14:17 NEB, emphasis added)

(12) These *Peace as Program* congregations are well situated to encourage the development of peace ministry in the ecumenical church. By active participation in local and regional ecumenical efforts, this type of congregation can further peace and unity in the church. The peacemaking ministries of the National Council of

Churches and the World Council of Churches are under attack by extreme rightwing Christians, anti-Communist fanatics, and interests associated with the military-industrial complex. This struggle is inevitable, but these congregations can join the struggle by interpreting ecumenical peacemaking efforts and by factual presentations of the reality of these ministries. The actions by the ecumenical bodies have engendered counteraction, and the tension provides unique opportunities for reflection on the meaning of church participation in peacemaking.

Probably most American Christian churches are represented in the *Peace as Present* and *Peace as Program* types. All of the activities just described also characterize the third type, *Peace as Political Policy* congregations. The public identity of this type of congregation seems to be growing. The cooperation and commitment of both the laity and the pastor or clerical staff is needed to bring congregations into a self-conscious position as peace activist congregations. Congregations have come to a point, usually over a number of years, where their life-style and confessions imply a clear yes to the priority of peacemaking and a clear no to militarism. Churches that have actively participated in the sanctuary movement to shelter Central American refugees are of this type as are those that regularly communicate with governing officials about peace and justice concerns. The latter type of action is within the normal recognized political process, the former action is a matter of resistance to governmental policy. These congregations tend to emphasize different actions as they approach the resistance to government policy stage, but they also display some common marks, including the twelve actions just mentioned. They also share the next three actions:

(13) These *Peace as Political Policy* congregations have recognized and taught that war in most cases is basically immoral. They have been unequivocal in rejecting reliance on weapons of mass destruction. This teaching and preaching in these churches has been consistent to the point that some Christians of the *Peace as Present* persuasion have sought out other Christian communities. They have generally managed to unite their Christian pacifists and realists to develop public church actions to oppose specific forms of militarism.

(14) These congregations have joined in revitalizing a Christian commitment to democratic politics of participation, debate, and petition. They have seen the church as having a role in the American political process, and they have welcomed campaigns like the nuclear

freeze, and programs to communicate with Congress on nuclear weapons, Central America, and South Africa. Politicians from different parties and persuasions are asked to participate in forums and educational programs in these churches.

(15) These congregations understand the role of voluntary associations in revitalizing American politics, and they have largely supported the formation of *shalom* communities and organizations. They teach and practice the financial support of peace organizations and a variety of peace workers because they know that the institutional strength and interest of the military-industrial-educational complex cannot be defeated by individual actions. Bread for the World is a good example of a public interest lobbying association whose politics are an expression of *shalom*. Food, not weapons, is a conviction that unites peace advocates in the northern countries and justice advocates in the southern countries. In many cities the United Nations Associations are vital groups that build public support for the U.N.'s contemporary work and keep alive models for international structures. The peace program of the World Federalist Association deserves support from Christians both for its immediate effects and for maintaining a vision of world order. Physicians for Social Responsibility have brought to many communities the message of the need to reverse the trend toward nuclear destruction. The doctors can witness on the consequences to health that few other groups could match. This vocational organizational pattern has spread to lawyers, teachers, business people, and scientists. Often these groups are led by Christian peacemakers, and usually coalitions with these groups are possible with congregations for political action. The *Peace as Political Policy* congregations tend to enthusiastically support the denominational staff, who are engaged in peacemaking ministries. They engage in church politics to keep the church focused on peacemaking in a public way.

Political Action and Resistance

The clear *no* to nuclear weapons and militarism can be expressed in both normal political action and in actions of resistance. The Christian peacemaker can move from resistance to political action and back again. There is no contradiction between engaging in civil disobedience and working for the election of public officials who will translate moral insight into public policy. It is natural and appropriate when released from jail, where one has been confined for conscientious civil disobedience, to engage in normal political activity, or to teach or to preach. A New York judge understood this at our arraignment for my illegally "sitting in" at the South Africa Embassy to the U.N. in New York City. He suggested a trial date in July and I demurred. He inquired about the reason for my wanting a later date, and I told him that I had my first teaching job at Morningside College in Sioux City, Iowa. He asked what I was going to teach, and I told him courses in ethics, history, and international relations. He replied kindly and ironically that he would not want the Iowans to be deprived of my teaching of ethics and international affairs. He set the trial date for the fall. There is no purely ethical preference for acts of resistance over normal politics. Both are means and the choice of means depends on the whole social-political situation as well as the ethical norms.

A congregation that legitimates acts of resistance to governmental authority will want to ground its resistance in its own ecclesiastical traditions and biblical authority. All of our denominational traditions have resisted unjust governmental authority on occasions. The biblical traditions likewise are full of accounts of people resisting authority to save life or to worship God.

The feminist contribution to peacemaking has highlighted two accounts of resistance. A favorite of mine is the Hebrew midwives' resistance to Pharaoh in Exodus 1:15-22. The Pharaoh's attempt to limit the growth of the Hebrew people by putting their male babies to death is thwarted by the trickery of the Hebrew midwives Shiphrah and Puah. They defy the command of their sovereign so that the children may live. In the next chapter the resistance to the Pharaoh spreads to his own royal household when his daughter disobeys him. Moses, saved by this defiance of the government, eventually leads his people into rebellion and freedom. In the Letter to the Hebrews, the New Testament author attributes both Moses' salvation from death and his leadership of resistance of the Egyptians to faith.

The second account so central to Judaism is that of Esther's bold breaking of the law in defying the Persian pogrom. Her statement of purpose to save her people represents one of the best protests that can be brought against law in order to save life: "I will go to the king, although it is against the law; and if I perish, I perish" (Esther 4:16 NEB).

The suffering of the New Testament central figures John the

Baptist, Jesus the Christ, Peter, Paul, Stephen, James, and John the author of Revelation all witness to their attempts to, in Peter's words, "obey God rather than men" (Acts 5:29). In them the shaking power of Mary's magnificat was revealed (Luke 1:46-55) as their testimony was proclaimed against the will of the authorities. Each congregation that will encourage actions like those enumerated in 16, 17, and 18, which follow, will need to carefully lay out its own understanding of biblical and church-historical support.

(16) The American-supported war efforts in Central America have called forth three unique forms of resistance by Christians to government policy. Sanctuary was initiated publicly by the Southside Presbyterian Church in Tucson, Arizona, in March 1982, on the anniversary of Archbishop Romero's assassination in El Salvador. Since that beginning, about three hundred Protestant and Roman Catholic churches in the United States have declared public sanctuary. Recently, cities have declared themselves to be sanctuary cities. Sanctuary is a Christian way to provide care and protection for refugees who are fleeing to the United States to escape violence in their own countries. As they have not been granted legal status to say in the United States, the policy of the Immigration and Naturalization Service (INC) has been to capture them and deport them back to El Salvador and Guatemala where they may be persecuted or killed or both. Churches supporting sanctuary are challenging the government in the name of the U.S. Refugee Acts of 1980 and the 1968 United Nations Protocol Relating to the Status of Refugees to protect these refugees. The conviction of sanctuary leaders has been appealed to higher courts, and the churches have sued the government in two sanctuary-related cases. Whatever the final court decisions, many of these congregations will continue to aid these poor brothers and sisters in Christ.,

Likewise through the Witness to Peace movement, many Christians have traveled to Nicaragua, with the support and sometimes commissioning by their churches, to oppose U.S.-supported invasions of Nicaragua. They have lived near the border in villages attacked by the Contras and prayed and studied with Nicaraguans.

About fifty thousand Americans have promised to engage in civil disobedience at governmental offices if the United States itself attacks Nicaragua. This marshaling of a nonviolent force before the invasion is supported by congregations and by ecumenical agencies of the churches.

(17) Another form of resistance encouraged by several congregations is the withdrawal of support from the military-industrial complex. Some congregations are supporting members who are engaged in tax resistance; in one small Presbyterian congregation in Atlanta, the majority of the members are not paying Federal income tax, many of them as an expression of resistance. Tax resistance takes many forms and the reactions of the U.S. government vary from case to case. Reducing taxable income is a legal way to avoid supporting the forces of militarism. Other tactics often slow down Internal Revenue Service collection, but hardly thwart the collection of the tax and penalties. Regardless of the pragmatic aspects of tax resistance, many Christians are led in conscience to resist in this manner and they deserve support from their congregations. Some Christians are leaving the military and industry because of the preparations of nuclear-war fighting strategies. The increasing militarization of the United States since 1980 has increased the crisis of conscience of many. Some of their decisions have been made without communal support, but others have received support from their Christian communities. Bishop Matthiesen of Amarillo, Texas, increased the visibility of this quiet form of resistance when he urged Catholics working at the Pantex nuclear assembly plant to consider leaving their jobs. In Colorado, a group of Presbyterians covenanted together as the New Earth Covenant Community with 10 percent of their income to assist people who out of conscience leave their work with weapons of mass destruction. Many Christians who have left the military or militarized industry have entered theological education seeking a new vocation where they can serve life.

Another form of withdrawal of support is the increasing church practice of noninvestment in firms heavily into armaments, especially nuclear armament production. This is on the borderline of tactics of churches in the *Peace as Program* type and the *Peace as Political Policy* type. The withdrawal of investments, with public education as to why in conscience such withdrawals are necessary, becomes a political act. If it is done quietly, with only interchurch discussion, it has less public impact.

(18) These congregations can encourage members to participate in public demonstrations and protests of various kinds. Congregations can support both legal and civilly disobedient forms of public action like marches, rallies, public worship, sit-ins, symbolic blocking of entrances to plants, and so forth. They can also lend support to peace movement actions by financial contributions, public legitimation,

interpretation, providing meeting rooms, and sometimes by initiating the protest. Each action of course has to be weighed by the responsible decision-making body in the church for its pragmatic, educational, and symbolic value. During the struggle for civil rights, rallies were often modeled on black church services and led by black clergy. During the war in Vietnam, worship services of activist churches were held against the war and for God in churches and in public places. The present crisis, which threatens all of life, must certainly receive more and more public witness by congregations dedicated to the love of God and neighbor. The nature of the church as a public gathering of Christians impels those who understand peace as political policy into public-communal action.

There are, of course, hundreds more actions to be taken in the peacemaking struggle. These eighteen, arranged for three types of churches, are only suggestions. They are recommendations growing out of personal experience in congregations. They are practical, since peacemaking can be embodied in the churches. Finally the peacemaking work has to persuade the Christian churches if there is to be peace. Peacemaking is not to be confined to the churches. It is the social necessity of the world. The churches both model and act for peacemaking. The conversion of the churches to peacemaking will in itself move the world close to peacemaking. The work of peacemaking, of course, moves beyond the churches to diverse financial institutions, various forms of government, and a plurality of creeds.

A word on the goal of peacemaking for the churches is needed. Jonathan Schell has proposed two different goals. In *The Fate of the Earth*, he argued for the necessity of world government. In *Abolition* he regards world government as impractical and he argues for the goal of total abolition of nuclear weapons. Both goals seem unfeasible until the major outstanding conflicts between the Soviet Union and the United States are relegated to insignificance. No nation will disarm its major weapons system or share a mutual government before understanding is improved. Mutual understanding, negotiation, and a détente involving heavy mutual economic interdependence needs to precede complete abolition of nuclear weapons or the evolution of international structures. Therefore, knowledge of the other, negotiating skills, and a will for mutual good remain as they always have, requirements for avoiding war.

The judgments about a freeze on nuclear weapons production, or a comprehensive test-ban treaty, or nuclear-free zones, or the elimination of undeveloped systems, or the rejection of the Strategic Defense Initiative, or major reductions in armaments are more positive. These are negotiable given the will to decide bilaterally to decrease the terror. Jesus' example of two kings approaching armed conflict did not recommend building more weapons, it did not urge world government, and it did not call for disarmament. He recommended negotiations (Luke 14:31-32). Diplomacy remains the solvent for handling conflict. Peace diplomacy will require the world's best talents and a turn away from militarism. Such a development of peace diplomacy requires the deepening of peacemaking in the country so that peacemaking-political leaders find sufficient public support.

The Christian vision or goal is of the kingdom of God, a reign of peace and justice, not of one without the other. Until that time, the penultimate goals of massive cuts in armaments, the development of international structures of order, and increasing social justice for the poor will need to be fought for in the political arena, and the church's peacemaking policy makes an indispensable contribution.

The important thing is to begin to act in everything we do as peacemakers. Micah told us 2,700 years ago what needed to be done: "He has showed you, O [humanity], what is good; and what does the Lord require of you but to do justice, and to love kindness, and to walk humbly with your God?" (Micah 6:8).

NOTES

PREFACE

1. Hans Morgenthau was a Jew, not a Christian. I have included his thought under this category because of his association with self-confessed Christian realists like Reinhold Niebuhr and Kenneth Thompson. He delivered his tribute to Niebuhr in the Cathedral of St. John the Divine recognizing Niebuhr as the greatest living political philosopher. Other Christian realists, e.g., John C. Bennett and Roger L. Shinn, utilized his thought as did Niebuhr. Niebuhr referred to Morgenthau as a "non-Christian realist friend" who did not agree with all of Niebuhr's theological convictions. "An Interview with Reinhold Niebuhr," *Christianity and Crisis* (March 17, 1969), p. 51. A further claim to at least honorary membership in this group rests in Kenneth Thompson, a Christian, telling me that Hans Morgenthau was the God-father of his second son, Paul.
2. *Peacemaking: The Believers' Calling* (New York: Office of the General Assembly, U.P.C.U.S.A., 1980).
3. *In Defense of Creation: The Nuclear Crisis and a Just Peace* (Nashville: Graded Press, 1986).
4. *A Just Peace Church* (New York: United Church Press, 1986).
5. *The Challenge of Peace: God's Promise and Our Response* (Washington, D.C.: National Conference of Catholic Bishops, 1983).
6. Dan Lawson, "A Study of the Pacifist Controversy in the Brethren Church" (an unpublished paper in the Doctor of Ministry program of Pittsburgh Theological Seminary, June 30, 1987).

I. PEACEMAKING AND WAR

1. Jonathan Schell, *The Fate of the Earth* (New York: Alfred A. Knopf, 1982).
2. Carl Sagan, "Nuclear War and Climatic Catastrophe: Some Policy Implications," *Foreign Affairs* (Winter 1983-84), pp. 257-92.
3. Paul Tillich, *The Systematic Theology*, 1 (Chicago: University of Chicago Press, 1952), p. 12.
4. Ibid., p. 49.
5. Ibid., p. 48.
6. Gustavo Gutiérrez, *A Theology of Liberation* (Maryknoll, N.Y.: Orbis Books, 1973), p. 13.

7. Tillich, *Systematic Theology*, 1, p. 14.
8. Benjamin F. Trueblood, "Peace Movements," *The New Schaff-Herzog Encyclopaedia of Religious Knowledge* (New York: Funk and Wagnalls, 1910), p. 430.
9. R. L. Ottley, "Peace," *Encyclopaedia of Religion and Ethics*, 9 (New York: Charles Scribner's Sons, 1917), p. 701.
10. Gerhard von Rad, "Shalom in the Old Testament," in Gerhard Kittel, *Theological Dictionary of the New Testament*, 3 (Grand Rapids: Wm. B. Eerdmans Publishing Co., 1964), p. 406.
11. Ibid., p. 405.
12. Werner Foerster, "Peace in the New Testament," in Gerhard Kittel, *Theological Dictionary of the New Testament*, 3 (Grand Rapids: Wm. B. Eerdmans Publishing Co., 1964), p. 412.
13. Ibid., p. 419.
14. Ibid.
15. Kenneth N. Waltz, *Man, the State and War: A Theoretical Analysis* (New York: Columbia University Press, 1959).
16. D. N. Premnath, "The Process of Latifundialization Mirrored in Isaiah 5:8-10," an unpublished faculty research seminar paper, January 30, 1985, United Theological College, Bangalore, India, p. 7.
17. Ibid., p. 11.

II. CHRISTIAN REALISM AND PEACEMAKING

1. Niebuhr's disapproval of Calvinist tendencies toward biblicism and legalism obscured his debt to John Calvin himself and especially to book IV, chapter 20 of John Calvin's *Institutes*.
2. Hans J. Morgenthau, *Politics Among Nations: The Struggle for Power and Peace* (New York: Alfred A. Knopf, 1967).
3. "Caribbean Blunder," *Christianity and Crisis* vol. 25, no. 9 (May 31, 1965): pp. 113-14.
4. John M. Swomley, Jr., *American Empire: The Political Ethics of Twentieth Century Conquest* (London: Macmillan, 1970), p. 34.
5. *Christianity and Crisis* 29 (August 4, 1969).
6. "After Sputnik and Explorer," *Christianity and Crisis* (March 4, 1958), reprinted in Ernest W. Lefever, *The World Crisis and American Responsibility* (New York: Association Press, 1958), p. 126.
7. "The Limits of Military Power," *The New Leader* (May 30, 1955), reprinted in Lefever, *The World Crisis*.
8. "American Hegemony and the Prospects for Peace," *Faith and Politics* (New York: George Braziller, 1968), p. 215.
9. Ibid., p. 211.
10. Ibid., p. 203.
11. Ibid., p. 236.
12. Ibid., p. 218.
13. *Reinhold Niebuhr: Prophet to Politicians* (Washington: University Press of America, 1981), pp. 207-10.
14. Swomley, *American Empire*, p. 35.
15. "An Interview with Reinhold Niebuhr," *Christianity and Crisis* 29 (March 17, 1969): 51.
16. Ibid.
17. Ibid.

18. "Peace Through Cultural Co-operation," *Christianity and Crisis* (October 17, 1949), reprinted in Lefever, *The World Crisis.*
19. Hans J. Morgenthau, *Politics Among Nations* (New York: Alfred A. Knopf, 1967), p. 374.
20. Ibid., pp. 540-45.
21. George F. Kennan, *The Fateful Alliance: France, Russia and the Coming of the First World War* (New York: Pantheon Books, 1984), p. 258.
22. George F. Kennan, *The Nuclear Delusion* (New York: Pantheon Books, 1982), p. 187.
23. Barton Gellman, *Contending with Kennan* (New York: Praeger Publishers, 1984).
24. Kennan, *The Nuclear Delusion*, pp. 206-7.
25. For a fuller discussion of my observations of the Soviet Union see: Ronald Stone, "Christian Realism and the Russians" in Beverly Harrison, et al. (eds.), *The Public Vocation of Christian Ethics* (New York: Pilgrim Press, 1986).

III. THE ETHICS OF PEACEMAKING

1. "The Report of the Public Hearing on Nuclear Weapons and Disarmament Organized by the World Council of Churches," in Paul Abrecht and Ninan Koshy (eds.) *Before It's Too Late* (Geneva: World Council of Churches, 1983), p. 31.
2. Edward Schillebeeckx, in Abrecht and Koshy, *Before It's Too Late*, p. 89.
3. Somen Das, "Anticipating the Future—Nuclear Holocaust," (Bangalore: University Scholar Seminar, unpublished paper, April 12, 1984), p. 4. Emphasis added.
4. *In Defense of Creation: The Nuclear Crisis and a Just Peace* (First Draft of United Methodist bishops, 1986), pp. 17-19.
5. Edward L. Long, Jr., "The Mandate to Seek a Just Peace" in Ronald H. Stone and Dana Wilbanks, *The Peacemaking Struggle: Militarism and Resistance* (Lanham, Md.: University Press of America, 1985), pp. 29-41.
6. Michael Walzer, *Exodus and Revolution* (New York: Basic Books, 1985), p. 149. Quotation from W. D. Davies, *The Territorial Dimension of Judaism*, (Berkeley: University of California Press, 1982), p. 60.

IV. REALISM, HUMAN RIGHTS, AND FOREIGN POLICY

1. The "Universal Declaration of Human Rights" itself refers to inalienable rights, barbarous acts, freedom of speech and belief, freedom from fear and want, rule of law, and the development of good relations among nations. Its words are very American and its tradition is secular liberalism, but that is rooted in deeper religious traditions particularly of covenant.
2. Kana Mitra, "Human Rights in Hinduism" in Arlene Swidler (ed.) *Human Rights in Religious Traditions* (New York: Pilgrim Press, 1982), pp. 77-84.
3. Pontifical Commission "Justice et Pax," *The Church and Human Rights* (Vatican City, 1975).
4. Ronald Dworkin, *Taking Rights Seriously* (Cambridge: Harvard University Press, 1978).
5. A. I. Melden, *Rights and Persons* (Berkeley: University of California Press, 1977).
6. Max L. Stackhouse, *Creeds, Society, and Human Rights: A Study in Three Cultures* (Grand Rapids: Wm. B. Eerdmans Pub. Co., 1984).

7. Stanley S. Harakas, "Human Rights: An Eastern Orthodox Perspective" in Swidler, *Human Rights*, pp. 17-18.
8. Egon Schwelb, "Human Rights," *International Encyclopedia of the Social Sciences* (New York: Macmillan, 1968), pp. 540-45.
9. See Robert N. Bellah, et al., *Habits of the Heart* (Berkeley: University of California Press, 1985) for a profound development of the social cost of the loss of social meaning.
10. Reinhold Niebuhr, "Preface" in *What Are Human Rights* by Maurice C. Cranston (New York: Basic Books, 1963), pp. v-viii.
11. Reinhold Niebuhr, "Freedom" in *Faith and Politics*. Ronald H. Stone, ed. (New York: George Braziller, 1968), p. 81.
12. Niebuhr, "Liberty and Equality" in *Faith and Politics*, p. 195.
13. Reinhold Niebuhr and Paul E. Sigmund, *The Democratic Experience: Past and Prospects* (New York: Frederick A. Praeger, 1969), pp. 81-82.
14. "The Social Myths in the Cold War" and "A Question of Priorities," *Faith and Politics*, pp. 223-44, 261-68.
15. Michael Novak, "Human Rights," Human Rights Conference, Kalamazoo College (April 26, 1978), pp. 6-7.
16. Lefever, "The Trivialization of Human Rights," *Policy Review* (Winter 1978), pp. 11-26.
17. Ibid., p. 13.
18. Ibid., p. 23.
19. Ibid., p. 26.
20. President Jimmy Carter, University of Notre Dame, May 22, 1977, as quoted in *The New York Times* (May 23, 1977), p. 12.
21. News Conference, Washington, D.C. (June 13, 1977), as quoted in *The New York Times* (June 14, 1977), p. 24.
22. Speech in Newcastle-upon-Tyne, United Kingdom (May 6, 1977), as quoted in *Los Angeles Times* (May 7, 1977), p. 18.
23. E. Brooks Holifield, "The Three Strands of Jimmy Carter's Religion," *The New Republic* 174 (June 5, 1976): 15-17.
24. June Bingham, "Carter, Castro and Reinhold Niebuhr," *The Christian Century* 94 (September 14, 1977): 775-76.
25. William Lee Miller, *Yankee from Georgia: The Emergence of Jimmy Carter* (New York: Times Books, 1978), pp. 201-47.
26. Ernest W. Lefever, "Niebuhr and the World Crisis," *The World Crisis and American Responsibility* (New York: Association Press, 1958), p. 4.
27. Lefever, "The Rights Standard," *The New York Times* (January 24, 1977).
28. Lefever, "The Trivialization of Human Rights," *Policy Review* (Winter 1978), p. 11.
29. Ibid., pp. 17, 18, 23.
30. Hearings Before the Committee on Foreign Relations, United States Senate (May 18 and 19, June 4 and 5, 1981), p. 76.
31. Ibid., p. 506.
32. Ibid., p. 505.
33. "Human Rights and National Security: An American Perspective," Agana, Guam (September 25-27, 1981), p. 1. Ernest Lefever has very generously provided several of his papers on human rights to the author.
34. Ibid., p. 2.
35. Ibid.
36. Ibid., p. 8.
37. The lowest argument I've seen was on a sheet Ernest Lefever sent me prepared by

the staff of the American Council for Co-ordinated Action, Inc. It described the propaganda campaign against Lefever as a " 'Reichstag Fire' kind of propaganda campaign." It portrayed Lefever as a victim of those seeking to promote worldwide socialism. The objectives of his opponents were assumed including the intent to "protect Marxist regions from charges of human rights violations."

38. A *Conversation with Michael Novak and Richard Schifter* (Washington, D.C.: American Enterprise Institute for Public Policy Research, 1981), pp. 24-25.
39. Ibid., p. 7.
40. Michael Novak and Richard Schifter, *Rethinking Human Rights* (Washington, D.C.: The Foundation for Democratic Education, 1981).
41. Stackhouse, *Creeds, Society, and Human Rights*, p. ix.

V. THE JUSTIFIABLE WAR TRADITION

1. Henry Paolucci, ed., *The Political Writings of St. Augustine* (Chicago: Henry Regnery Company, 1962), p. 182.
2. Roland H. Bainton, *Christian Attitudes Toward War and Peace* (Nashville/New York: Abingdon Press, 1960), p. 97. This exposition of Augustine on the just war follows Bainton except on one point. Paul Ramsey has the better of the argument, as he argues that no requirement for the absolute justice residing with one side in a war was suggested by Augustine. Paul Ramsey, *War and the Christian Conscience* (Durham, N.C.: Duke University Press, 1961), pp. 15-33
3. Hebert A. Deane, *The Political and Social Ideas of St. Augustine* (New York: Columbia University Press, 1963).
4. James T. Johnson, quoted in Donald L. Davidson, *Nuclear Weapons and the American Churches* (Boulder, Col.: Westview Press, Strategic Studies Institute, U.S. Army War College, Carlisle Barracks, Pa., 1983), p. 5.
5. Ibid.
6. A. P. D. Entreves, ed., *Aquinas Selected Political Writings* (Oxford: Basil Blackwell, 1965), pp. 159, 161.
7. Joseph C. McKenna "Ethics and War: A Catholic View," *American Political Science Review* (September 1960).
8. John Calvin, *Institutes of the Christian Religion* (1559), ed. John T. McNeill, trans. Ford Lewis Battles (Philadelphia: Westminster Press, 1960), II. viii. 39.
9. Ibid., IV. xx. 12.
10. Edward LeRoy Long, Jr., *War and Conscience in America* (Philadelphia: Westminster Press, 1968), pp. 24-29.
11. "Winning Peace," text of the statement issued by the French bishops, Lourdes, November 8, 1983. Translated by the Press and Information Service of the French Embassy, Washington, D.C., p. 9.
12. *In Defense of Creation* (first draft, revised), p. 15.
13. Recommended critiques of "Star Wars" include: John Tirman (ed.), *The Fallacy of Star Wars: Based on Studies Conducted by the Union of Concerned Scientists* (New York: Vintage Books, 1984). Robert W. Bowman, *Star Wars: Defense or Death Star* (Potomac, Md.: Institute for Space and Security Studies, 1985). Patricia M. Mische, *Star Wars and the State of Our Souls* (Minneapolis: Winston Press, 1985).
14. Kenneth W. Kemp, "The Moral Case for the Strategic Defense Initiative" in Malhan M. Wakin (ed.) *War, Morality and the Military Profession* (Boulder, Col.: Westview Press, 1986), pp. 509-16.
15. Ronald Reagan quoted in ibid., p. 514, from Hugh Sidney, "The Presidency" *Time* (January 28, 1985), p. 29.

16. See William J. Broad, "The Secrets of Soviet Star Wars," *The New York Times Magazine* (June 28, 1987), pp. 22-28.
17. Carl Sagan, "Nuclear War and Climatic Catastrophe: Some Policy Implications," *Foreign Affairs* (Winter 1983-84), pp. 257-92.
18. James Gleick, "Less Drastic Theory Emerges on Freezing After Nuclear War," *The New York Times* (June 22, 1986), p. Y13.
19. Calvin, *Institutes*, II. viii. 39.

VI. REVOLUTION AND COUNTERREVOLUTION
IN CENTRAL AMERICA

1. I have adapted the just-war criteria in an earlier study on the ethics of revolution. See *Realism and Hope* (Washington, D.C.: University Press of America, 1977).
2. See *Realism and Hope* for interpretations of Gregory VII, Martin Luther, and John Knox as revolutionaries.
3. Tillich, *Systematic Theology*, 3 (Chicago: University of Chicago Press, 1963), p. 344.
4. Ibid., p. 388.
5. For an essay critical of the Sandinista church policy, see "The Church in Nicaragua Under Attack from Within and Without," *Religion in Communist Lands* 12 (Spring 1984): 42-54.
6. *Christianity and Crisis* 43 (January 23, 1984): 518.
7. Jacobo Timerman "A Time for Straight Folk," *Newsweek* (March 11, 1985), p. 4.
8. "Nicaragua: A War of Words," *Newsweek* (March 11, 1985), p. 35.
9. Vic Jameson, "News," Presbyterian Office of Information (February 21, 1984), no. 8109, p. 1.
10. See William Sloane Coffin, "Sanctuary for Refugees and Ourselves," *Christianity and Crisis* 45 (March 18, 1985): 75-76.
11. See Ronald H. Stone, "A Black Liberation Theology from Jamaica," *The Christian Century* (July 31, 1974).
12. Harvey Cox, "Who Is Ernesto Cardenal?" *Christianity and Crisis* 43 (April 4, 1983): 126.
13. Gustavo Gutiérrez, *A Theology of Liberation* (Maryknoll, N.Y.: Orbis Books, 1973), pp. 27, 88, 111.
14. See José Porfirio Mirando, *Marx and the Bible* (Maryknoll, N.Y.: Orbis Books, 1974), pp. xiii-xviii.
15. Gutiérrez, *A Theology of Liberation*, pp. 29-32.
16. Gustavo Gutiérrez, *The Power of the Poor in History* (Maryknoll, N.Y.: Orbis Books, 1983), p. 135. Emphasis added.
17. Ibid., pp. ix, 45, 78, 85, 186, 192.
18. *The New York Times* (March 24, 1985), p. 7.
19. I am indebted to Allan Boesak for showing me how the "Courage to be" arises to oppose the threat of the oppressor. His reflections on dignity put words to the obvious experience of the members of the *communidade de base* I have talked with. See Allan Boesak, *Farewell to Innocence: A Socio-Ethical Study on Black Theology and Black Power* (Maryknoll, N.Y.: Orbis Books, 1977), p. 49.
20. Dennis P. McCann, *Christian Realism and Liberation Theology* (Maryknoll, N.Y.: Orbis Books, 1981), p. 231.
21. "Instruction on Christian Freedom and Liberation," *The New York Times* (April 6, 1986), p. Y10.

VII. DEVELOPMENT: THE INDIAN EXAMPLE

1. Richard Fox, *Reinhold Niebuhr: A Biography* (New York: Pantheon Books, 1985), p. 130.

2. Quoted in Gunnar Myrdal, *The Asian Drama*, 1 (London: Allen Lane, 1968), p. 704.

3. Jay Dubashi, "Budget: The Rajiv Model," *India Today* (April 15, 1985), p. 114.

4. Ibid., p. 82.

5. *Bhopal Gas Tragedy* (New Delhi: Society for Delhi Science Forum, 1985).

6. *Origins* 14 (November 15, 1984), p. 372.

7. Committee on a Just Political Economy, Presbyterian Church (U.S.A.), *Toward a Just Caring and Dynamic Political Economy* (January 22, 1985), p. 6.

8. *Churches and the Transnational Corporations* (Geneva: World Council of Churches, 1983), p. 11.

9. "Rise of the Middle Class," *India Today* 10 (December 31, 1985): 74. Emphasis added.

10. Larry L. Rasmussen and Bruce Birch, *Bible and Ethics in the Christian Life* (Minneapolis: Augsburg Publishing House, 1978), p. 181.

11. *Origins*, p. 375.

12. "The Church and Transnational Corporations," *Church and Society* 74 (March-April 1984).

13. Ibid., p. 38.

14. Richard J. Barnet and Ronald E. Muller, *Global Reach* (New York: Simon and Schuster, 1974).

15. S. Swaminathan, "Dilemmas in Development" J. T. K. Daniel and R. Gopalan (eds.) *A Vision for India Tomorrow* (Madras: Madras Christian College, 1984).

16. Charles Elliott, *The Development Debate* (London: SCM Press, 1971).

17. Devaki Jain, *Development as if Women Mattered or Can Women Build a New Paradigm* (New Delhi: Institute of Social Studies Trust, 1983).

18. Ibid., p. 23.

19. Gunar Myrdal, *The Asian Drama: An Inquiry into the Poverty of Nations*, p 680. The five-point outline of factors resisting development is drawn from *The Asian Drama*. The discussion is updated by references to developments since the book's 1968 publication.

20. M. M. Thomas, *Response to Tyranny* (New Delhi: George Matthew, 1979), pp. 33-34.

21. Geevarghese Mar Osthathios, *The Sin of Being Rich in a Poor World* (Madras: The Christian Literature Society, 1983), p. 68.

22. John Mohan Razu, *An Ethical Evaluation of the Impact of the Selected TNCs or Development in India* (Bangalore: Unpublished M.Th. Thesis, 1984).

23. V. Guari Shankar, *Taming the Giants: Transnational Corporations* (New Delhi: Vidya Vahini, 1980), pp. 208-9.

24. G. Shiri, *Karnataka: Christians and Politics* (Madras: The Christian Literature Society, 1978).

25. Jain, *Development*, pp. 30-31.

26. The odds against development are great. Yet biblical faith is full of promises of the overcoming of degradation. On the world scale, 1984 was a year of economic growth and some parameters of Indian economy show progress. There is room for the guarded hopes that are intended in the paper.

    India does not need a pessimistic reading by an American theologian. My intention is to be realistic; development can be advanced. The realism of an Indian scholar, K. C. Alexander, needs to be noted. The paragraph quoted is from a paper sent to the University Scholars Seminar at United Theological College (April 12, 1984). Though the paper is titled "The Future of the Harijans in India," this paragraph deals with development in India:

    Almost four decades after India's independence, and six Five Year Plans, about half of the population live below poverty line, unable to meet even basic calorie requirements. In 1981, the per capita per day food production in India was equivalent to 2,000 calories only. The Census of 1981 indicated that 65 percent of the population was illiterate, unable to write their names. . . . As a result, the scope for percolation of modern knowledge and scientific practices to rural areas is extremely limited.

VIII. RESPONSE TO RELIGIOUS ROOTS OF TERRORISM

1. Leon Wieseltier, "What Went Wrong? An Appraisal of Reagan's Foreign Policy," *The New York Times Magazine* (December 7, 1986), p. 137.
2. Harold Lasswell, "Terrorism and the Political Process," *Terrorism: An International Journal* 1 (1978), p. 255, quoted in Martha Crenshaw, ed., *Terrorism, Legitimacy and Power* (Middletown, Conn.: Wesleyan University Press, 1983), p. 3.
3. Several cases are detailed in *Washington Newsletter* 491 (May 1986): 3.
4. See Douglas Mitchell, "Extremism and the Paramilitary Movement" in Ronald Stone and Dana Wilbanks (eds.), *The Peacemaking Struggle: Militarism and Resistance* (Lanham, Md.: University Press of America, 1985), pp. 275-94.
5. Connor Cruise O'Brien, "Thinking about Terrorism," *The Atlantic Monthly* 257 (June 1986): 65.
6. Statistics from Moojan Momen, *An Introduction to Shi'i Islam* (New Haven, Conn.: Yale University Press, 1985), p. 282.
7. Ibid., p. 283.
8. Ibid., p. 286.
9. Roy Mottahedeh, *The Mantle of the Prophet* (New York: Simon and Schuster, 1985), p. 183.
10. Ibid., p. 177.
11. Documentation and help in interpretation from Robin Wright, *Sacred Rage* (New York: Simon and Schuster, 1985).
12. Wright, *Sacred Rage*, p. 271.
13. Daniel Goleman, "The Roots of Terrorism," *The New York Times* (September 2, 1986), pp. 19, 22.
14. Though the work of relating justifiable-unjustifiable war criteria to the issues of terrorism has begun, its results so far leave more precision to be desired. See, for example, John Dugard, "International Terrorism and the Just War," in David C. Rappoport and Yonah Alexander (eds.), *The Morality of Terrorism: Religious and Secular Justifications* (New York: Pergamon Press, 1982).
15. Ali A. Mazrui, "A Third World Perspective," *Ethics and International Affairs* 1 (1987), p. 18.
16. Max Stackhouse, "Torture, Terrorism and Theology: The Need for a Universal Ethic," *The Christian Century* 103 (October 8, 1986): 861-63.

IX. RELATIONS WITH THE RUSSIANS

1. "Superpower Ethics," reprinted from *Ethics and International Affairs* 1, 1987.
2. There are many examples of this change. A recent one in which the author's perspective is so attacked is Lloyd Billingsley, "Foreign Palsy: A Critique of Moral Equivalence" in Ted M. Dorman, *Peacemaking or Resistance?* (Nashville: Presbyterians for Democracy and Religious Freedom, 1986), pp. 37-47.
3. The debate between Richard Pipes, others, and George Kennan is captured in a collection of essays. See Martin F. Herz, ed., *Decline of the West?* (Washington, D.C.: Georgetown University, 1978).

4. Ronald H. Stone, "An Interview with Reinhold Niebuhr," *Christianity and Crisis* 39 (March 17, 1969): 48-49.
5. The seminar papers and lectures were published: See Robert K. German (ed.), *The Future of U.S.-U.S.S.R. Relations: Lessons from Forty Years Without World War* (Austin: University of Texas, 1986).
6. Andrey A. Kokoshin is Deputy Director, Institute for the USA and Canada, Academy of Sciences of the U.S.S.R. Moscow. The quotation is from Robert K. German (ed.), *The Future of U.S.-U.S.S.R. Relations*, p. 144.
7. John Lewis Gaddis is Professor of History, Ohio University. The quotation is from Robert K. German (ed.), *The Future of U.S.-U.S.S.R. Relations*, p. 115.
8. Unfortunately, Mikhail Gorbachev's farsighted plans for accelerating his country's socioeconomic development are still packaged in the wrappings of expectations of the West's decline. His program for the Communist Party of the Soviet Union includes charges like the following: "No 'modifications' and maneuvers by modern capitalism have rendered invalid or can render invalid the laws of its development or can overcome the acute antagonism between labor and capital, between monopolies and society or can bring the historically doomed capitalist system out of its all-permeating crisis." "The Program of the Communist Party of the Soviet Union," in *The Challenges of Our Time: Disarmament and Social Progress* (New York: International Publishers, 1986), p. 169. Similar statement from Mikhail Gorbachev, p. 12.
9. George Kennan, "The Sources of Soviet Conduct," *Foreign Affairs* (Spring 1987), a reprint of a July 1947 essay by X, p. 868.
10. W. W. Rostow, "On Ending the Cold War," *Foreign Affairs* 65 (Spring 1987): 831-51.
11. Philip Taubman, "Architect of Soviet Change," *The New York Times* (July 10, 1987), pp. 25, 27.
12. Arkady N. Schevchenko, "Gorbachev or Not, Reform Will Stay," *The New York Times* (July 10, 1987), p. 23.
13. George W. Breslauer, "The Nature of Soviet Politics and the Gorbachev Leadership" in Alexander Dallin and Condoleezzo Rice, *The Gorbachev Era* (Stanford. The Stanford Alumni Association, 1986), p. 22.
14. Wassily Leontief, "Will Free Enterprise Sell in Moscow," Review of Marshall I. Goldman, *Gorbachev's Challenge* in *The New York Times Book Review* (June 21, 1987), p. 9.
15. Martin Gorbus, "Allowing Publication of a Journal," *The New York Times* (July 23, 1987), p. 23.
16. *Soviet Military Power, 1987* (Washington, D.C.: Department of Defense, 1987).
17. The figures are for 1983 from *World Military Expenditures and Arms Transfers, 1985* (Washington: Arms Control and Disarmament Agency, 1985).
18. *Soviet Military Power, 1987*.
19. See William J. Broad, "The Secret of Soviet Stars," *The New York Times Magazine* (June 28, 1987), pp. 22, 24, 25, 28.
20. Mikhail Gorbachev, *Perestroika: New Thinking for Our Country and the World* (New York: Harper & Row, Publishers, 1987).
21. The recent reality of the Soviet Union is a necessary prerequisite for understanding the current changes. *The Gulag Archipelago* is hard reading. Solzhenitsyn himself recognizes how hard it is to continue to wade through the state terrorism he describes. He begins volume three: "To those readers who have found the moral strength to overcome the darkness and suffering of the first two volumes, the third volume will disclose a space of freedom and struggle." Aleksandr I. Solzhenitsyn, *The Gulag Archipelago Three* (New York: Perennial Library, 1976), p. xi.

INDEX OF SCRIPTURAL REFERENCES

Genesis
35:5.................................. 138

Exodus
1:15-22.............................. 172
20:2-3............................... 149
23:27................................ 138

Leviticus
19:18................................. 61

Deuteronomy
15......................... 126, 127

I Kings
5:12................................... 24

Esther
4:16.................................. 176

Job
41....................................138

Psalms
20:7.................................... 52
103:6................................. 137

Isaiah
1............................ 28, 29, 30
2............................27, 28, 138
3.......................................29
5:8-10................................ 31
5:26-30.............................. 29
32:17-18............................ 127
54:10................................. 24
65:20-25............................ 129

Jeremiah
29:7....................................57
29:11.................................. 57

Ezekiel
13:16................................. 24

Daniel....................................56

Hosea
10:10-14.............................. 52

Joel..................................... 56

Amos
1:9....................................... 69
9:13-14................................57

Micah
6:8.....................................176

Zechariah
9:10.................................... 24

Matthew
5:9..................................... 25
22:37-40............................. 61
25:35-36............................. 128
26:11................................. 126

Mark
12......................................61

Luke
1:78-80...........................34, 35
1:46-55.............................. 173

Luke (cont.)
10... 61
21:11.. 138

Acts
2:45.. 62
4:35.. 62
5:29.. 173

Romans
5:1... 53
5:22-24... 57
8:31.. 52
12:18... 25
13...138

I Corinthians
13:13... 48
16:14... 61

Galatians
5:14..61

James
2:26..55
4:1-20............................... 55, 56

Revelation
16:16.. 56

GENERAL INDEX

A *Just Peace Church*, 12
Abrahms, Elliot, 84
Advisory Council on Church and Society, 13
Afghanistan, 46, 52, 145, 161
Alliance for Progress, 31
Aquinas, Thomas, 68, 71, 89-92
Arias peace plan, 121
Aristotelian philosophy, 150
Armageddon, 55, 56
Augustine, 35, 41, 48, 87-90, 93, 166

Bangalore, 13, 137
Bennett, John C., 9
Berrigan, Daniel, 111
Bethlehem, 17
Bhagavad Gita, 26
Bhopal, 13, 123
Birch, Bruce, 126-27
bishops: American Roman Catholic, 96;
French Roman Catholic, 97;
United Methodist, 97-98
Boesak, Allan, 117, 168
Boff, Leonardo, 117
Bread for the World, 171
Brethren Church, 12
Brezhnev, Leonid, 9

Caesar, 34, 35, 102
Calvin, John, 33, 92, 93, 101, 103
Cardenal, Ernesto, 110-12
Carter, Jimmy, 66, 73, 77-79, 138, 143
Central America, 102-21, 173
Chamberlain, Neville, 17
China, 18, 153, 161

Christ, Jesus, 20, 34, 35, 43, 53, 67, 87, 94, 126, 150, 172
Christian realism, 9, 10, 11, 33-47, 79, 94, 119, 122, 145-47, 149
Chrysostom, John, 71
church policy, 165-76
cold war, 36-47, 153
communidade de base, 117
communism, 43, 46, 51, 62, 78
Cone, James, 168
Constantine, 34, 102
Contras, 120, 139
counterrevolution, 102-21
Cox, Harvey, 111
Cuba, 77, 107, 161
Czechoslovakia, 17

Das, Somen, 60
deterrence, 11, 94-98, 140
development, 122-37, 164
Dharma Sutra, 67
diplomacy, 44, 176
disarmament, 96, 176
Dulles, Allen, 104, 105
Dulles, John Foster, 39, 104, 105
Dworkin, Ronald, 68

El Salvador, 104-9, 173
Elliott, Charles, 129, 135
Elmhurst College, 13
Episcopal Church, 97
Erikson, Erik, 52
eschatology, 57, 58
Ethiopia, 18, 161

faith, 48-55

Fate of the Earth, 19, 175
feminist, 172

Gandhi, Indira, 14
Gandhi, Mahatma, 67, 68, 130, 166
Gandhi, Rajiv, 123, 132
Gellman, Barton, 46
Germany, 50, 82
Geyer, Alan, 167
Glasnost, 160
God, 22-26, 28, 47, 48, 53, 54, 61, 77, 87, 137, 176
Gorbachev, Mikhail, 9, 43, 46, 156, 157, 161, 162
Gulag Archipelago, 163
Gutiérrez, Gustavo, 20, 111, 112, 114, 115, 120, 168

Hinduism, 49, 50, 116, 131
Hitler, Adolf, 17
hope, 48, 55-61
human rights, 66-85, 128, 158
humanity, 19, 20, 77

Idea of the Holy, 26
idolatry, 48-52
Iliad, 26
Immigration and Naturalization Service, 109, 173
In Defense of Creation, 12
India, 18, 31, 49, 51, 107, 116, 122-36, 161
Iran, 18, 46, 138-50
Iraq, 144, 145, 161
Islam, 138-50
Israel, 17, 18, 30, 148

Jain, Devaki, 129, 130
Jefferson, Thomas, 74, 104
Jew(s), 17, 159
John XXIII, 63
John Paul II, 113, 125
Johnson, James T., 90
Judaism, 172
Jurgensmeyer, Mark, 122, 166
just peace, 63-64, 164
justice, 11, 62, 75, 76, 125-28, 176
justifiable war, 86-102

Kennan, George, 9, 10, 33-47, 153, 168
Kerala, 122, 135
Khomeini, the Ayatollah Ruhollah, 141-44

Khruschev, Nikita, 9, 139
King, Martin Luther, Jr., 58, 59, 68
Kingdom of God, 57, 59, 60, 64, 176
Kissinger Commission, 106, 120

LaFeber, Walter, 37
Lefever, Ernest, 72-82
Lewis, Dean, 14
liberation theology, 21, 30, 111-20, 168
Long, Edward L., Jr., 64
love, 48, 61-63
Luther, Martin, 103

McCann, Dennis, 118
Machiavelli, Niccolo, 33
Man, the State and War, 27
Manley, Michael, 110
Marx, Karl, 115
Marxism, 113, 115, 117, 119, 167
Marxist, 112, 113, 117, 119
Marxist analysis, 113, 118
Marxist philosopher, 32
Melden, A. I., 110
militarism, 18, 59, 172
More, Thomas, 33
Morgenthau, Hans J., 9, 33-47
Moslem, 17, 49
Myrdal, Gunar, 130-32, 136

Napoleon, Bonaparte, 144
National Council of Churches, 11
Nazism, 10, 151
neoconservative, 10, 11, 41
New Jersey, 146, 147
Nicaragua, 18, 104-21, 173
Niebuhr, Reinhold, 10, 29, 30, 33-47, 67, 73, 74-77, 80, 120, 122
North Atlantic Treaty Organization, 160-62
Novak, Michael, 13, 66, 77, 83, 84

Otto, Rudolph, 26

Pakistan, 18, 161
peace, 11, 66, 164
peace as political policy, 167-70
peace as present, 166, 167
peace as program, 170-75
peace churches, 12
peacemaking, 9, 11, 12, 23, 25, 66, 137, 145, 147, 151, 164-76
Peacemaking: The Believer's Calling, 11
perestroika, 156, 163

Pipes, Richard, 152
Pittsburgh Theological Seminary, 12, 13, 111
Plato, 22, 93
Politics Among Nations, 36, 43
poverty, 51, 104, 115, 125, 127, 130-32, 137
power, 38, 39, 120, 152
Prague, 17, 32
Premnath, D. N., 31
Presbyterian Church (U.S.), 11
public demonstrations, 174

Rasmussen, Larry, 126-27
Ratzinger, Joseph, 119
Rauschenbusch, Walter, 10
Reagan, Ronald, 55, 67, 99, 100, 138, 162
realism, 138, 139, 153
Realism and Hope, 12
resistance, 11, 171-75
revolution, 102-21
Rockefeller commission, 110
Rome, 34-35, 56-70
Ruether, Rosemary, 168

Sagan, Carl, 19, 101
SALT II, 99, 161
sanctuary, 173
Sandinista regime, 106, 107, 114
satyagraha, 64
Schell, Jonathan, 19, 47, 175
Schifter, Richard, 83, 84
Shah Pahlavi, 142-44, 148
shalom, 11, 17, 24, 25, 61, 125, 166, 171
Shia Islam, 141-50
Shiite crusade, 141-45
Sikhs, 13, 141
Singh, V. P., 123, 133
slavery, 72
Smylie, Robert, 13, 167
Soelle, Dorothee, 169
Solzhenitsyn, Aleksandr, 60
Somoza family, 106
Somoza regime, 107
Soviet Military Power, 160-63
Soviet Union, 10, 18, 37-40, 45, 46, 107, 151-64

Stackhouse, Max, 70, 122, 150
Stalin, Joseph, 32
Strategic Defense Initiative, 98, 99
Sunni, 141
Swomley, John M., 37, 40

tax resistance, 174
terrorism, 138-50
The Asian Drama, 130-32
The Challenge of Peace, 12, 96
theology, 19-23, 107
Thomas, M. M., 122, 131
Tillich, Paul, 19, 20, 21, 22, 62, 103, 104
transnational corporations, 127-36

UNESCO, 42
Union Carbide, 123, 124
Union Theological Seminary, 22, 76, 122
United Church of Christ, 67, 165
United Kingdom, 18, 82, 130
United Methodist Church, 11, 12, 61, 97, 98
United Nations, 27, 42, 71, 73
United Presbyterian Church (U.S.A.), 11, 125

Vietnam, 36, 38, 40, 59, 76

Waltz, Kenneth, 27, 30, 32
Walzer, Michael, 65, 94
war, 26-32, 38, 41, 44, 64, 86-101, 109
Warsaw Pact, 160
Weber, Max, 117, 137
Weinberger, Caspar, 55
Whitehead, Alfred North, 29, 30
Wilbanks, Dana, 14, 166, 167
Witness to Peace, 173
women's organizations, 136
World Council of Churches, 11, 71, 125
World Court, 64, 119
World Federalist Association, 171
world government, 42, 64
World War I, 52, 152
World War II, 51, 152
Wright, Robin, 148

Young, Andrew, 67, 73